THE TRUTH ABOUT GOD

FRANZ KIEKEBEN

THE TRUTH
ABOUT
GOD

PARTHENON BOOKS

ISBN-13: 978-1512271409

ISBN-10: 1512271403

CONTENTS

INTRODUCTION

And ye shall know the truth, and the truth shall make you free.

– John 8:32

The question of God's existence is an extremely important one. On that, at least, just about everyone can agree. After all, theists and atheists have vastly different conceptions of reality. The view that an immensely powerful spiritual being controls the universe itself is not just any old belief: it is a strange and extraordinary hypothesis. It affects a person's entire outlook on existence, typically determining many of one's attitudes toward life, meaning, and morality. If it were true, it would change everything. No wonder, then, that it has been a major concern of philosophers for more than two millennia. And yet, in spite of its importance, the existence of God no longer appears to be the main topic of discussion between believers and nonbelievers. The popular atheist books of the last decade or so have dealt primarily with the evils of religion – in particular, its ties with war and terrorism, and its fundamental irrationality. The opposition's rejoinders likewise concentrated on the consequences of belief, arguing, among other things, that religion played an essential role in the development of science and in the spread of human rights (neither of which is the case, of course, but that's a different matter). God's existence, when considered at all, tended to be treated very much as a secondary issue. Perhaps the feeling many have is that most of what can be said about it has already been said, and that rehashing the same old, well-known arguments is simply beside the point.

In fact, however, recent developments in science and philosophy have given new life to this age-old question and have made it once again a lively subject for debate. Disputes over such claims as that the universe is finely tuned for the existence of life and that naturalism cannot account for morality continue to attract the attention of scientists, philosophers, theologians, and others. In addition to all this, there are new arguments to be made on the side of nonbelief. An up-to-date investigation of the main points, and of the issues underlying them, is therefore entirely justified.

Moreover, atheism – although it is more popular and more conspicuous than ever before – is not being defended as vigorously as it could be. Most people who call themselves atheists these days merely claim a lack of belief in God, rather than positive disbelief. And whereas arguing against the existence of God isn't all that uncommon, professing *knowledge* of his non-existence is much rarer – while claiming to have a decisive argument against theism is almost unheard of.

It is a fairly simple matter to argue for the nonexistence of the biblical deity, or of the all-powerful, all-knowing, perfectly good being that most people believe in. But most atheists would say that where the general concept of God is concerned, nothing conclusive can be said. The great majority are willing to allow that God in this sense is at best highly improbable; they do not believe in him, but neither do they think his existence can be ruled out entirely. The central chapter in Dawkins's *The God Delusion* is titled "Why there almost certainly is no God," not why there definitely isn't one, while the ads in the recent Atheist Bus Campaign in Britain merely stated that "there's *probably* no God." The view of just about every atheist, in other words, is that the existence of God is not, strictly speaking, impossible, and thus that no definitive demonstration of atheism is available.

I want to challenge this view. It seems to me that we can conclude with approximately the same level of certainty that no deity whatsoever exists, whether it be the God of Christianity, the God of Islam, the deistic God, or any other. We can even say this with respect to the gods of polytheistic religions. And the reason is that no such beings *can* exist, period. I admit this is a surprising claim. Even if it is possible to disprove the existence of certain gods, getting rid of all of them at once may appear to be completely out of the question. But in fact the argument I make is relatively short and simple, and can be understood even without any background on this topic.

The claim I am making is not, it must be said, quite as out of the ordinary as the above might suggest. Many atheistic philosophers these days in fact will say that they know no gods whatsoever exist – just as we know that other mythical beings do not exist. I take things one step further, however: it's not just that the gods are sufficiently improbable that we can know they aren't there; it's that they are *impossible*. In this respect, then, the claim I am making is far stronger, and perhaps unique. It is also sure to be controversial – but then again, in this area, what claim isn't?

The argument that no gods are even possible is found in chapter seven. However, the book isn't by any means limited to this one idea. The fact is that one cannot make a persuasive case in support of atheism without first addressing the actual beliefs of theists. Abstract philosophical arguments will fail to convince anyone certain that Jesus was raised from the dead. For this reason, more specific issues will be considered first. In the pages that follow, then, readers will find, in addition to the above refutation of theism, criticisms of the Bible and of the supposed historical evidence for the Jesus of scripture, a new version of the problem of evil, reasons to reject the immateriality of the soul, and much, much more. The strongest proofs *for* the existence of God – such as the fine-tuning argument and the Kalam cosmological argument – as well as the most common objections to atheism will also be dealt with.

Although this book is not primarily an attack on religion – there are no discussions of pedophile priests, Islamic terrorists, or greedy televangelists here – that does not mean religion isn't criticized. It does however mean that such criticism is for the most part limited to what is relevant to the book's central question, that of the existence of God. This criticism is also limited to Christianity (and by extension Judaism), which may very well lead to complaints on the part of some. Why not similarly object to Islam, Hinduism, Sikhism, the theistic forms of Buddhism, or any of the many other religions out there? The answer should be obvious: Christianity is the view held by the majority of individuals in our culture, and thus the one that religious readers of this book are the most likely to hold. It should go without saying that comparable criticisms could be made of other faiths.

The additional material in defense of atheism included throughout the book also means that believers who reject the argument in chapter seven will probably still have to contend with problems that apply to their particular views. Not everything hinges on that one argument, and even without it we have very strong reasons for disbelieving in God. My hope is that with this book, readers will have at their disposal a comprehensive defense of atheism that at the same time is firmly centered on its most important questions.

1

ATHEISM AND GOD

We are all atheists about most of the gods that humanity has ever believed in. Some of us just go one god further.

– Richard Dawkins, *The God Delusion*

Interest in atheism is on the rise. Both on television and in print, news stories featuring atheists and atheist organizations are more common than they have been in years, and non-religious viewpoints are now often mentioned alongside religious ones. Secular events such as the 2012 Reason Rally held in Washington manage to draw crowds in the tens of thousands,[1] while young people are rejecting the faith of their parents and embracing nonbelief in ever-increasing numbers. It all began a decade ago, when books critical of religion by the so-called "new atheists" turned into surprise bestsellers – and it doesn't appear like it's going to be ending any time soon. The godless have never been so visible, or godlessness so popular.

And yet in spite of all this – or perhaps to some extent because of it – "atheism" remains a bad word: those who do not believe in God are still viewed with suspicion, disdain, or outright hostility by a majority of the population. This is not just an impression many of us happen to have. Recent polls show that Americans distrust atheists more than they distrust any other main demographic group, including Muslims,[2] and would sooner vote for a homosexual than for an atheist for president.[3] According to one study, even *rapists* are often thought more trustworthy![4] Nor is it that uncommon for those who deny God's existence to be shunned by neighbors, to lose their jobs, or even to receive death threats.[5] As a consequence, if you are a nonbeliever, chances are you are still in the closet. But why should that be? Why are atheists the targets of the one remaining "acceptable" form of prejudice?

The main culprit is, of course, religion itself, which has traditionally demonized the nonbeliever above everyone else. The Psalms famously state of atheists that "they are corrupt, they do abominable deeds; there is none that does good."[6] Hebrews 3:12 warned us against having "an evil, unbelieving heart," while Jesus said that "those who do not believe are condemned already."[7] Echoing such sentiments, St. Thomas Aquinas held "the sin of unbelief" to be "greater than any sin that occurs in the perversion of morals"[8] and recommended the death penalty for offenders. Nor are judgments of this kind limited to ancient and medieval times. The popular contemporary evangelist Ravi Zacharias may not go as far as Aquinas in practice, but he does think that to effectively tell God you don't need him is worse than being a murderer – worse, in fact, than being a serial killer.[9] Lack of faith is the ultimate evil. That's one way religions ensure that they maintain a following. And even though some progress has been made and attacks on nonbelievers are not as frequent as they used to be, the feeling that atheism is in some way unseemly persists.

There are also historical reasons why Americans in particular view atheism in a bad light. Ever since its earliest days, when Puritan John Winthrop described her as like a "city upon a hill" and a beacon of Christianity to the rest of the world, many saw this nation as having a special relationship with the Almighty. Some even thought of her as the new Israel. During the Cold War, when the enemy consisted of the "godless Communists," the feeling intensified. "In God we trust" became our official motto, "under God" was added to the Pledge of Allegiance, and godlessness became, more than ever before, associated with anti-Americanism. It should not be surprising, then, that for many people atheism immediately suggests a number of negative things.

As far as most believers are concerned, if someone is an atheist then he must be a radical liberal, or worse. He wants to stop the words "Merry Christmas" from ever being uttered in public again, and the sight of a nativity scene probably makes him angry. He must not love his country, at least not if his country is America – for how could someone love this country and at the same time deny that there is a God? Worst of all, an atheist is more likely than not an immoral person, a libertine who desires to satisfy his or her own desires above all else, and who thinks that nothing is greater than him or herself.

If you don't subscribe to any of these caricatures, you might think that I'm exaggerating. Unfortunately, however, such views are common, and it's not at all difficult to find evidence for them. Here is a small sampling from just the last few years:

In *What's So Great about Christianity*, well-known author and commentator Dinesh D'Souza writes that "the perennial appeal of atheism [is that it] liberates us for the pleasures of sin and depravity" and adds that "when an atheist gives elaborate justifications for why God does not exist and why traditional morality is an illusion, he is very likely thinking of his sex organs."[10]

On CNN's *Paula Zahn Now*, during a panel discussion following a story about discrimination against atheists, journalist Karen Hunter called the story "ridiculous" and said that atheists "need to shut up." Another member of the panel, columnist Debbie Schlussel, agreed: "freedom of religion doesn't mean freedom *from* religion... it's obnoxious, and they do need to shut up."[11]

In 2008, Illinois State Representative Monique Davis had the following choice words for an atheist testifying before a government committee: "What you have to spew and spread is extremely dangerous ... it's dangerous for our children to even know that your philosophy exists! This is the land of Lincoln, where people believe in God! Get out of that seat ... You have no right to be here! We believe in something. You believe in destroying! You believe in destroying what this state was built upon."[12]

And a recent book on the new atheist phenomenon by religious philosopher James Spiegel claims that "atheism is not the result of objective assessment of evidence, but of stubborn disobedience; it does not arise from the careful application of reason but from willful rebellion. Atheism is the suppression of truth by wickedness, the cognitive consequence of immorality. In short, it is *sin* that is the mother of unbelief."[13]

To many religious people, lack of faith appears to be a rejection of the heavenly father. As the Bible puts it, "the fool has said in his heart 'There is no God'."[14] Notice that it's in his *heart*, not in his mind, that the "fool" has reached his conclusion. The atheist, then, must not want to believe in a higher power. Maybe he even hates God. And since God is perfect in his goodness, the atheist's decision must be immoral, and ultimately based on a desire to escape God's all-seeing nature and judgment. Why else would anyone reject a loving Creator and his gift of eternal life?

All of these ideas are, of course, complete nonsense. But if one is going to be writing about atheism, it is important to make it clear from the start exactly what atheism is and why all of the above are misconceptions. Fortunately, this isn't too difficult a task, for the meaning of atheism is fairly straightforward. There are a couple of minor complications involved, but leaving those aside for the moment, we can say that an atheist is simply someone who believes that there are no gods. A *theist*, by contrast, is, in the widest sense of the word, someone who believes that there is at least one god. That is the entire difference between them. Their disagreement is simply an intellectual disagreement about the nature of reality. As such, it is in principle no different from the disagreement between, for instance, those who believe the universe is infinite and those who believe it is finite, or between those who accept homeopathy and those who do not. It is a disagreement, in other words, over a matter of fact: either there is at least one god or there are none. Atheism makes no other claims. It does not have a particular moral point of view, or a particular political point of view, or anything else. It is certainly possible for an atheist to reject political liberalism, to be vehemently opposed to communism, or to be a very patriotic American. It is also possible for an atheist to be kind to his neighbors, donate to charities, and be truthful on his income tax return. More importantly, an atheist is not someone who hates God or who has made a decision to turn away from God. If one does not believe there is a God in the first place, then one cannot turn away from him: *there is no God to turn away from.*

This isn't to say that there are no atheists who are influenced by a desire that there be no higher power to judge them. My point is merely that that is not part of what it means to be an atheist. Some individuals come to accept Christ because they drink too much, cheat on their spouses, or commit crimes, and find in religion the motivation to stop. It does not follow that to be a Christian is to be a recovering alcoholic, former adulterer, or repentant criminal. Similarly, some atheists may refuse to consider religion because they want to continue drinking, gambling, or what have you, and are afraid that if they come to accept God they will no longer be able to do those things. In fact, this is an all-too-common feature of religious conversion stories. Lee Strobel, a former atheist who is now an author of popular books defending the faith, claims that he originally had "a strong motivation to ignore" evidence for Christianity – namely, "a self-serving and immoral lifestyle that I would be compelled to abandon if I were ever to change my views and become a follower of Jesus."[15] But of course one can be an atheist for different reasons. Most nonreligious individuals aren't irresponsible hedonists and self-serving immoralists. What such conversion stories suggest, perhaps, is that those who are unbelievers for the wrong reason are more likely to eventually find religion. Those who have considered the evidence and who actually understand the grounds justifying the secular worldview are much less likely to convert. They aren't nearly as liable to fall for the illusions of faith.

I am also not denying that the majority of atheists, at least in the West, are liberals. That this is the case should not be too surprising: people who are more progressive in their attitudes toward politics are also more likely to break with tradition on social matters. It would be unusual to find a social conservative who is also an atheist (and would in fact be impossible if we define "social conservatism" as requiring some type of theistic belief). But an atheist can certainly be a fiscal conservative, and many are. Furthermore, not all atheists are particularly troubled by expressions of religious belief in the public sphere. Not all are engaged, or even all that interested, in political activism, such as the attempt to remove "In God we trust" from U.S. currency or to "unpatriotically" change the Pledge of Allegiance back to its original form.

At this point, many believers may be thinking to themselves that there are other reasons to be concerned about atheism. Maybe atheists can be well-meaning, even moral, people. Maybe they come from all walks of life and from a variety of cultural and political backgrounds. But however well-intentioned, they are a danger, for they might convince others that there is no God. And those who do not believe in God are condemned to hell fire. So atheists may be putting people in worse than mortal danger: they may be endangering people's immortal souls!

Notice, however, that the above concern is itself ultimately based on the idea that nonbelief is a sin – in other words, on the idea that atheism is a rejection of God. And that, in turn, is based on the assumption that there is ample evidence for God's existence and that therefore there is no excuse for failing to believe. That is the assumption I'll be challenging in this book. I do not think we have good grounds for believing in God. In fact, it's even worse than that. Not only is there no actual evidence for the existence of God, there is quite a bit of evidence – some of it conclusive – *against* the existence of God. Or so I shall argue.

DEFINING ONE'S TERMS

Above, I said that an atheist is someone who believes that there are no gods. In recent times, however, it has become common among nonbelievers to define atheism more broadly. Rather than limiting the term to those who specifically reject the existence of any god, the new trend is to apply it to anyone who does not positively believe in a god – anyone, in other words, who is a nontheist. Consider agnosticism. Agnostics claim not to know whether there is a God. Hence, they (usually) neither believe nor disbelieve in him, but instead suspend their judgment. An agnostic does not *believe that* there are no gods, so he does not count as an atheist by the definition used in this book. But he obviously *lacks* belief in any god. Thus, he is an atheist on the wider meaning of the term. So for that matter are infants (much to the horror of some parents), since infants do not yet have the conceptual ability to believe in a god.

This broadening of the concept of atheism seems to be getting more popular. It is common to see debates on the existence of God in which the purported atheist maintains that he does not have to provide evidence that there isn't a deity: the onus of proof, he states, is entirely on the side of theism, for only the theist is making a positive claim. Now, if the atheist is merely someone who fails to believe for lack of evidence, then of course all he has to show is that the theist's arguments aren't convincing; he does not have to, in addition, present any arguments of his own. No wonder, then, that this view is popular among nonbelievers: it makes things considerably easier! And of course it's fine if people want to argue this way. Nevertheless, this broad definition is not the traditional meaning of the word. And besides, as already mentioned, I'll be arguing that there are reasons for positively claiming that God does not exist, which means that I'll be arguing for the narrower type of atheism. Therefore, it makes sense for me to use the term in its more traditional sense.

There is a second minor complication regarding the meaning of atheism (and of theism, for that matter). Atheists believe that there are no gods, whereas theists believe there is at least one god. But what, exactly, are gods? This isn't an easy question to answer. To begin with, the word usually means one thing for polytheists and another for monotheists. If we say – along with most polytheists – that a god is any agent with superhuman powers who controls some aspect of the world, traditional Christianity would appear to be a type of polytheism, since, in addition to the one supreme being, it affirms the existence of various angels and demons. But of course Christianity does not regard any of these lesser beings as true gods. Satan may *want* to be God – and is in fact described in the Bible as being "the god of this world"[16] – but he is no more divine than you or I. The term "god," in its strict sense, is therefore narrower for monotheists, and is reserved for the highest among all supernatural entities. This supreme being is the one that we are primarily concerned with in this book, and the one I will refer to by the capitalized word "God." But further clarification is needed, of course, as this term can designate almost anything, from an anthropomorphic deity with a long, flowing white beard to a timeless immaterial entity to the physical universe itself. If we are to discuss God's existence, then, we must first provide some additional details.

In most works of this kind, God is defined in a rather restrictive way. One recent book states that he is a spiritual, personal being who is all-powerful, all-knowing, perfectly good, omnipresent, immutable, necessary, interested in humans, and the creator of everything other than himself. It follows that anyone who believes in a being with all of the above attributes except, say, immutability, is not, according to the definition, a true (mono)theist. But of course such an individual ought to be considered a theist. The definition given is far too specific. At the other extreme there are definitions that are much too inclusive. Some theologians, for instance, define God as "ultimate reality," or as "the ground of all being," or some such thing. That way, they can cleverly rule out the very possibility of atheism, since atheists, like everyone else, presumably accept the existence of ultimate reality and of the ground of being. Such definitions, however, besides being too broad and too vague, fail to capture what theists really believe.

What, then, must someone accept in order to qualify as a monotheist? It seems reasonable to claim that, at a minimum, one must hold that there is *a conscious being who is in some sense ultimately responsible for the existence of everything else* – either because that being created everything else, sustains everything else, or both. This, then, is what I will mean by the term "God." (I will have a bit more to say about what "ultimate responsibility" implies later on, in chapter seven.) The claim that there is such an entity is what, at the most fundamental level, distinguishes those who believe from those who do not. Most people believe much more than that about their God, of course. They also believe that he is all-powerful, or that he is eternal, or that one part of him assumed human form as Jesus of Nazareth – or perhaps all of these things and many others besides – and in what follows I will consider some of the most important of these additional claims made about God. At the end of the day, however, it will be the above basic understanding of the supreme being that will primarily concern us, for that is the core concept shared by monotheists of every stripe, whether Muslim, Jewish, deist, or anything else.[*]

---

[*] From this point on I will generally use "theism" to refer to monotheism.

IS ATHEISM A RELIGION?

Religious believers often maintain that atheism is "just another religion." This is a somewhat ironic claim, since it is intended critically, and thus makes it appear that the believer disapproves of religion. What is almost certainly meant, however, is that atheists are really just like everyone else, and are therefore wrong to criticize other people for their (admittedly unproven) beliefs. As some put it, to accept atheism, one must have faith that there is no God. Some go further, and claim that it actually takes *greater* faith to be an atheist.

Whether or not atheism is a religion depends, of course, on what is meant by "religion." On just about any reasonable definition, however, atheism cannot possibly qualify. A religion is a complex system of teachings. It usually includes some views concerning the purpose of existence, whether of the universe as a whole or of each individual life. It almost always prescribes certain practices, such as rituals and rules pertaining to diet and attire. And it is ultimately based on faith. Atheism fails to qualify as a religion on every single one of these counts. It is not a complex set of beliefs, but rather a single claim: that there are no gods. It does not state that there is an overall purpose to things – and in fact suggests the exact opposite. It does not stipulate what one should or shouldn't do. And, contrary to what many maintain, it is not a type of faith. This last point, more than the others, requires some elaboration.

A belief held on faith is one that is not dependent on reason or observation, and furthermore, that reassures or comforts the believer. As the Bible puts it, faith is "the substance of things hoped for, the evidence of things not seen."[17] Both components are important: faith signifies hope, and implies belief even in the absence of evidence. Hence, even if all atheists believed without justification, atheism could not be classified as a faith for the simple reason that it is not about any particular hope or desire. But in addition, atheism is more often than not based on the available evidence: people have reasons for rejecting deities. So atheism is not a type of faith in either respect.

The impression that one must have faith in order to disbelieve is probably due to the (generally accepted) idea that the nonexistence of God, at least in the most general sense of that term, cannot be decisively demonstrated. If proof isn't available, then − many conclude − the only thing left must be faith. But that is a misconception. The error here can most clearly be seen if we consider a different question, such as whether or not unicorns are real. One cannot prove that in the entire history of the world there have never been any unicorns, and yet, in spite of this, our belief that they are mere fantasy does not rely on faith. We have good reasons for rejecting their existence. For one thing, there is a very plausible hypothesis as to where the unicorn legend began (with the rhino, which many in ancient times had heard of but never seen), and clear evidence as to where the idea of a spiral horn originated (with the spiral tusk of the narwhal whale, which sometimes washes up on shores). Furthermore, had there been an equine species with a single horn, we would probably have some hard evidence of that fact. It follows that it is perfectly reasonable to claim, based on what we do know, that unicorns have never existed. And what goes for the nonexistence of unicorns goes for many, many other things. Proof is not always required. One can reasonably claim to know that something does not exist even if all one has is evidence that that thing is very unlikely. But in addition, as already mentioned, I will be arguing in this book that the existence of God is not just improbable, but impossible – and that makes the claim that atheism is a faith even more obviously false. When one has a conclusive demonstration, faith cannot play a role at all.

Atheism, then, is not a type of religion; it is not a faith. My portrayal of religious belief as based on faith *instead of reason* may not sit well with some readers, however. Surely religious people also can, and often do, offer justifications for their views? Of course. Theologians and religious philosophers spend much of their time doing just that. (They may not be *good* reasons, but that's a different matter.) A belief that is based on faith does not necessarily mean one that cannot also be justified. Evidence may be found that supports it. But none of this contradicts my central point, which is that religious doctrines are not *dependent on* reason and evidence. That is not how they originally came about, and that is not why the religious ultimately accept them. The faithful may appeal to reasons in support of their beliefs, but the beliefs come first, independently of such reasons. It might further clarify things if I point out that, on the interpretation of religion just presented, it doesn't even follow that all *theists* are religious. Someone who thinks there is a God solely because she is convinced that that is the best explanation for the existence and characteristics of the universe, is not religious. Deists such as Thomas Jefferson and Benjamin Franklin come to mind. They rejected religious dogmas but nevertheless concluded there must be an intelligent creator, for that was the only way they could account for the fact that we live in an orderly, lawful universe. Contrast their outlook with that of someone who already accepts the existence of God and only appeals to reasons when challenged to defend her view. The latter type of individual would have believed in God even without the reasons, and that is what makes her a person of faith. It follows that atheism is not a religion, *and neither is theism.*

SHOULD ONE BE CONCERNED ABOUT ATHEISM?

Whether or not they consider it a type of faith, there are those who doubt that it is ever wise to argue on behalf of atheism. For even if it is true that there is no God, might it not be a bad idea to convince people of that fact? Perhaps religion makes people happier, healthier, and more highly moral than they would otherwise be, and if so, the proselytizing atheist is doing humankind a great disservice. After all, on the face of it, religion does seem to serve some purpose and to have a number of beneficial effects. For one thing, belief helps many people cope with some of the more difficult aspects of life. One very obvious example of this concerns death. We are the only animal that understands the concept of death, and that fact alone goes a long way toward explaining the phenomenon of religion. Natural disasters, disease, and human misery in general – all things that, if anything, should make us *doubt* the existence of a benevolent creator – contribute to religious belief by creating a need for it. (The influence that religion has here is of course limited. If people accepted wholeheartedly the idea that the dead are in a better place, they wouldn't think of death as so tragic.)

Belief also helps in more subtle ways. Probably most of us at least sometimes feel that there is little point to anything we do. What is the purpose of it all? There certainly appears to be none. Thoughts of this kind even lead some to seek comfort in potentially harmful things, such as alcohol, drugs, or existentialism. But the believer – although she may not know exactly why – often *feels* that her life somehow has meaning because there is a God. Conversely, many believers think that to abandon their faith would be to lose all sense of purpose in their lives, and to feel nothing but emptiness and despair. Such people often claim they feel sorry for atheists; some even manage to be condescending about it.

Religion also functions as a tool for social cohesion and collective action, as well as a means by which individuals interact for their mutual benefit. This aspect of it may have had greater importance in earlier times, when more societies were to a significant extent defined by their religious identities, but in many ways it is still relevant. People sense that they are part of a unified community when they belong to this or that house of worship. And of course the role that religion plays in charitable work, especially in times of great need, ought to be recognized by everyone. Even the most diehard atheist should admit as much – though it must be said that many unfortunately do not.

Religion, then, serves a number of useful functions. However, many of these can almost certainly be achieved in other ways. In addition, it is undeniable that religion has many drawbacks as well. The "new atheist" books – which were initially motivated by the events of 9/11 – are primarily about the evils of faith. The terrorists responsible, after all, would not have acted as they did had they not been deeply religious. Their faith motivated them – at least in part – and gave them the courage to carry out their plans. As physicist and new atheist Victor Stenger succinctly put it, "Science flies us to the moon. Religion flies us into buildings."[18] And even though the new atheist books have been accused of greatly exaggerating the negative aspects of faith, even the most devout must admit that they make many good points as well.

Religion, as stated above, promotes social cohesion – having a shared belief system allows the members of a society to more readily feel they are part of the tribe – but the flip side of this is that it tends to turn anyone with incompatible views into the enemy. By defining itself in terms of its beliefs, the society comes to see competing belief systems as potential threats. Those within the society who fail to conform are regarded as dangerous, while other societies are more readily seen as alien or even subhuman. It shouldn't be surprising, then, that religion has led to a great deal of hatred, and a lot of blood has been spilled in its name. The 9/11 terrorist attacks are just one example of this. This is not to deny that the terrorist attacks, as well as such things as the Arab-Israeli conflict and the recent problems in Northern Ireland and Sri Lanka, also have political causes. They are certainly not just about religion. Nevertheless, the individuals involved in these conflicts identify themselves and their opponents primarily in terms of their religious affiliations. Thus, even if in some cases it is not the root cause, religion functions at least as a catalyst. Other well-known examples of faith-based violence include the persecution of Christians in ancient Rome, the Crusades, the Spanish Inquisition, the wars over the Reformation, the Salem witch trials, the war between Hindus and Muslims in India, and the various conflicts between the Sunnis and the Shia throughout the Arab world. But of course religious intolerance causes other harms as well. It has enslaved, and continues to enslave, millions who are unable to speak or act freely. Customs as barbaric as anything out of Deuteronomy persist even today. In certain parts of the world, for instance, women who are raped are, under Sharia Law, sometimes stoned to death for having had extramarital relations. In many of these same areas, apostasy is punishable by death – which is all the more absurd given that the majority of people do not even choose their religion in the first place, but have it forced upon them by their parents and by society. In at least seven nations one can still be executed for the "crime" of atheism. And, although this is not nearly as serious, religious belief continues – as has already been observed – to be a source of prejudice against nonbelievers even in the West. Finally, religious inflexibility prevents progress in many areas, sometimes with deadly consequences. The clearest example of this is the Catholic Church's opposition to contraception, which has almost certainly led to a very large number of deaths from HIV in the Third World. It is only relatively recently that Church policy on this issue has begun to change.

These are not the only problems associated with religion, but they are certainly sufficient to show that *at best* religion is a very mixed bag. In fact, from what has been considered so far, it seems pretty clear that its influence has overall been negative. But the believer might protest at this point that, in addition to the direct benefits of religion listed above, there is the indirect benefit it has had of keeping atheism's influence at bay. For, as many religionists have recently argued, perhaps atheism is guilty of far greater crimes still.

The examples of atheism's evils that are almost always brought up are those of Hitler and Stalin – with Mao and Pol Pot sometimes thrown in for good measure – and the conclusion one is supposed to draw is that abandoning religious morality can lead to the slaughter of millions. Now, the first thing to point out regarding this argument is that the example of Hitler isn't at all a good one. There isn't much evidence either way as to his religious views, but even if we grant that he was an atheist, we have to remember that most of his followers, including many of those in authority positions, were undoubtedly Christian. In addition, it is obvious that anti-Semitism has to a great extent been motivated by Christianity, which traditionally blamed the Jews for the death of Jesus. The majority of Jewish people rejected the idea that Jesus was the Messiah – a perfectly reasonable thing for them to do, given that Jesus was not a great military ruler who overthrew the Roman occupiers, but was instead executed like a common criminal. For Jesus's followers, however, such a rejection was unforgivable. Their attitude can be seen in such biblical passages as Mathew 27:25, which has the Jewish crowd exclaiming "His blood be on us, and on our children." In a papal bull from 1555, the Pope justified relegating the Jews to a ghetto because their "own guilt has consigned them to perpetual servitude."[19] Luther went even further than his Catholic rival, recommending "in honor of our Lord and of Christendom" that (among other things) their synagogues be burned, their houses destroyed, and their prayer books and valuables taken from them.[20] Hatred of the Jewish people, then, can hardly be attributed to atheism. But the religionist doesn't need Hitler to make his case anyway. Stalin was responsible for a greater number of deaths, and he was most definitely a nonbeliever who operated in a secular regime. Is atheism in this instance to blame, then?

The standard reply to this charge is that it wasn't Stalin's lack of belief in God that turned him into a tyrant: it was his adherence to an evil political philosophy, combined with a desire for personal power, that led to his atrocities. The only thing Stalin has in common with all other atheists is disbelief in God. Christians, on the other hand, share a whole set of beliefs with other Christians, including with those responsible for religious brutalities.

So when religious critics say things like "Christians must answer for the Inquisition, and atheists must answer for Stalin,"[21] they go too far. The Soviet leader presumably also did not believe in leprechauns. Must all leprechaun deniers answer for his crimes as well? To put it another way, atheism may sometimes be associated with undesirable policies, but it does not lead to them all on its own. Religions, on the other hand, are not merely incidentally linked to abuses of power: they often bring them about directly. When nonbelievers are regarded as evil and as a potential threat to those in control, one should in fact *expect* the Spanish Inquisition!

Still, many theists remain unconvinced. They are likely to point out that lack of religious belief was essential to the worldview of communist dictators – one cannot be a true Marxist and believe in God, after all. So lack of belief may not by itself give rise to totalitarian systems, but it is one way to make them possible. The basic idea, then, is that, by leaving religion behind, atheists unwittingly open the door to doctrines that view the government, or even the dictator, as the ultimate moral authority, and the result has been these widespread crimes against humanity. But is this a good argument? No, for at least a couple of reasons. In the first place, there are many highly atheistic societies in which the supposed terrible consequences of unbelief have not materialized. Japan, Norway, and Denmark are all among the least religious nations in the world right now, and yet not only are they democracies, they also have some of the lowest crime rates in the world. Sweden, Germany, France, and many other countries also have majorities that are irreligious. Obviously, it takes more than atheism to make the Gulag possible. (That such societies exist and function just fine also backs up the view, already mentioned above, that the majority of the supposed benefits of religion can be achieved in other ways.) Second, to suggest that religious morality has the power to prevent the kind of evil acts that Stalin committed is simply absurd. Here, the example of Hitler actually works against the theist's line of reasoning, for has already pointed out, Nazi Germany was not by any means an atheistic society. Even if Hitler was an atheist, why didn't the religious beliefs of other German government officials and military leaders interfere with his plans? German soldiers even had the slogan "God with us" imprinted on their belt buckles! To consider another example, is there any doubt that if Tomás de Torquemada, the infamous head of the Spanish Inquisition, had reason to murder millions instead of hundreds, he would have done so? And as to there ever actually being a reason for religion to kill in such great numbers, unfortunately that too is not out of the question: religiously motivated acts involving nuclear weapons might one day massacre as many as were massacred by atheist dictators. Even without such weapons religion has already contributed to the deaths of millions in numerous wars. In these respects, then, belief is no better – and is in fact almost certainly worse – than nonbelief.

One final thought on the reasonableness of advocating atheism: as their constant references to "the Truth" attest, the religious, like everyone else, wish to avoid falsehood. In fact, nearly everyone would rather face harsh facts than be comforted by pleasant lies – and I say this in spite of the fact that many of us obviously do believe such lies, for when we do, it is only subconsciously. No one *wants* their beliefs to be false. There is something rather unbecoming in preferring fantasy, however attractive it may be, to reality. After all, happiness is not the only thing that matters to us. We want love, friendship, experiences, knowledge, and other things, in part because they make us happy, but we do not want them for that reason alone: we want them for their own sake. That this is so can be seen by means of a simple thought experiment. If happiness were the only thing that mattered, we would all rather spend our lives in drug-induced bliss, hallucinating enjoyable experiences with imaginary friends in imaginary places. Yet given a choice between, on the one hand, a very contented dream state filled with wonderful illusions, and on the other, a normal, ordinary existence, nearly everyone would opt for the latter. Experiencing reality as it truly is, with actual human interaction, with awareness of our authentic surroundings – all of that matters a great deal to us. Reality and truth, then, are important in their own right. Happiness isn't the only thing.

Now, for some of us, abandoning religious belief might be a temporarily disorienting experience. It might make us somewhat unhappy to give up ideas and ways of thinking that we have been familiar with throughout our lives. But if we really *care* about the truth, if it is important for us to avoid deluding ourselves, then we should seek that truth, even when some potential cost is involved. And at any rate atheists aren't actually living lives of hopelessness and despair, as many suppose. One can be just as happy and fulfilled without belief in God. In fact, I have never met an atheist who wished he were religious. There simply is no reason to fear atheism.

2

CHRISTIAN

UNAPOLOGETICS

> Properly read, the Bible is the most potent
> force for atheism ever conceived.
>
> — Isaac Asimov

When asked why they believe in God, most people appeal to basic philosophical arguments. They might ask where everything came from if there is no God, or claim that the world is too complex to have arisen by mere chance. That at any rate is how people tend to justify their belief in a deity. It is obvious, however, that that's not why most believe in the first place: the real reason is religion. As far as most theists are concerned, then, merely presenting philosophical arguments against the existence of God isn't enough; a case for atheism won't be convincing unless the claims of religion are addressed – and addressing the claims of religion, in our society at least, means for the most part addressing those of the Christian tradition. In this and the next chapter we will therefore examine the evidence for and against Christianity.

Unfortunately, however, there isn't a single, unified set of beliefs comprising Christianity. People who call themselves Christian range from so-called inerrantists, who insist that every word in the Bible (at least as it was originally written) is true, to extreme liberals who in some cases aren't even real theists. In what follows, I will essentially ignore the liberal camp: their position, insofar as it is genuinely theistic, will be dealt with by later chapters. Here we will be concerned only with the beliefs of those who profess a more traditional type of Christianity. But neither do I want to limit my criticisms to the views of inerrantists – people who imagine the world is but a few thousand years old, that Adam and Eve were real individuals, and that there was once an actual worldwide flood. The criticisms that follow will of course apply to them – but they will apply to far less extreme positions as well.

The views I will take to be generally accepted by what I call traditional Christianity include the belief that God is morally perfect; that scripture is in some sense his divinely inspired word; that he sent Jesus to die for our sins and then raised him from dead; and – though this last one isn't nearly as essential – that some of his creatures end up in hell. Those in this traditional camp, then, may agree that many of the biblical stories aren't factual, but are there instead merely to teach some moral lesson. But of course even parts of the Bible that are held to be fictional must make sense: they must be free of contradiction and the morals they reflect must be admirable. Anything less and the claim of divine inspiration cannot reasonably be maintained. It follows that even the non-literal portions of scripture are open to criticism.

It's only logical for the believer to concede that at least some of scripture is fictional. After all, given what we know about the earth and its history, it is nothing short of crazy to insist on biblical inerrancy. As it turns out, however, the admission that there are nonfactual stories in scripture raises certain problems. That the good book features a talking donkey[22] may not in itself be troubling; it may be considered mere allegory. But the fact that ancient people interpreted such stories literally, and that many still do even today, *is* problematic. God would have known that for most of human history, just about everyone brought up on the Bible would believe tales of this sort. Thus, unless there is some justification for deceiving the ignorant and the credulous, God did something wrong. At the very least, the Bible fails in that it is not very clear. Often, apologists argue that what appear to be errors in scripture can be resolved provided we interpret things differently, and they then present a complex story to justify their interpretation. But why would God have made things so difficult in the first place? The Bible is supposed to be the primary means of spreading his message, and if so, it seems he could have done a better job. It makes no sense for him to have communicated with us in ways that are downright confusing. This *problem of unclarity*, as I'll call it, is something we will encounter a number of times throughout this discussion.

Another problem with the existence of biblical fiction is this. Every rational and educated person admits that much of the Bible is fable. But in that case, how can they be sure about those parts they do believe? Might they not be fictional as well? After all, the story of Christ is also meant to teach important moral lessons, and it does not have to be literal truth in order to do that. Throughout modern times, with advances in our knowledge, the number of biblical stories whose facticity is rejected has steadily grown. It wouldn't be surprising therefore if in a few hundred years the majority of Christians viewed the gospel accounts the same way that many already view Old Testament myths. The kind of liberal Christianity mentioned above may become a much more widespread phenomenon. And in fact, as inerrantists often point out, the claim that some parts of the Bible are fictional conflicts with the belief in the literal truth of certain other parts of the Bible. For instance, the story of Jonah, who survived for three days inside a "great fish," is thought by many to be a mere tale. However, Jesus himself, in Matthew 12:41, refers to it as if it were true. Inerrantists appeal to this as evidence of its veracity. As one of their Biblical scholars, Gleason Archer, put it, "Jesus did not take [the book of Jonah] to be a mere piece of fiction or allegory, as some would-be Evangelicals have suggested. Adherence to such a view is tantamount to a rejection of Christ's inerrancy and therefore of His deity."[23] In other words, if Jesus was God and believed Jonah spent three days inside a fish or whale, then Jonah must really have done so. Of course an alternative conclusion is that Jesus *wasn't* God: that would explain how he might have believed such obvious nonsense. Thus, the inerrantists' argument can easily backfire and be taken as a *reductio ad absurdum* of Christianity as a whole. If Jonah – or Adam and Eve, or Lot's wife turning into a pillar of salt – are fictional, then Jesus, who apparently thought otherwise, couldn't have been who he is claimed to be.

Difficulties with the Bible fall into three main categories. There are internal inconsistencies, that is, statements that contradict other statements in the Bible itself. There are simple falsehoods, especially of a scientific nature. And there are moral principles that modern-day readers do not accept – or at least that they would never accept coming from any other source – in spite of the fact that the devout must regard every principle in its pages as true. These things have been pointed out many times before, with little effect on believers. I will not, therefore, waste a lot of space repeating all of the same old criticisms. There are dozens of these, and merely listing them does little good. A more effective approach is to consider a few examples from each category and examine the various explanations that have been proposed for them. We can then contrast the religious interpretation of these things with the skeptical one. By doing so, we will be able to see that, whereas the skeptical explanations make perfectly good sense, the religious ones all fall short.

INTERNAL INCONSISTENCIES

An interesting thing regarding contradictions in the Bible is that one doesn't have to wait very long at all before coming across the first one: a blatant discrepancy is found right at the beginning. Chapter one of Genesis, the six day creation story, states that God made plants and animals before he made human beings: plants on the third day, aquatic and flying animals on the fifth, and land animals followed by people on the sixth (during the fourth day, he was, strangely enough, busy creating the rest of the entire universe). In chapter two, however, God creates Adam "when no plant of the field was yet in the earth and no herb of the field had yet sprung up – for the LORD God had not caused it to rain upon the earth, and there was no one to till the ground."[24] It is also after Adam that he creates non-human animals, as can be seen from the following passage: "And the LORD God said, 'It is not good that the man should be alone; I will make him an help meet for him.' And out of the ground the LORD God formed every beast of the field, and every fowl of the air; and brought them unto Adam..."[25] So when were human beings created, before or after other living things? There doesn't appear to be any satisfactory way to answer this question.

THE ORDER OF CREATION ACCORDING TO GENESIS 1 AND 2:

GENESIS 1	GENESIS 2
1. Plants	1. Humans
2. Animals	2. Plants
3. Humans	3. Animals

Now, there are those who maintain that, being omnipotent, God is able to do literally anything, including the logically impossible. According to this way of thinking (which we will have occasion to criticize later on), God could, if he wanted to, create square circles and married bachelors. He could bring it about that one plus one equals three, alter the past, and even make the Pope a protestant. I wouldn't be entirely surprised, therefore, if I heard it claimed that the first human being was created *both before and after* other living things. God works in mysterious ways. There are somewhat more reasonable explanations, however.

One way of resolving the problem, at least with regards to the animals, involves changing the tense in the translation of some of the passages, so as to make the creation of animals prior to the creation of Adam. This is the approach taken by the translators of the New

International Version. Thus, verses 18 and 19 are changed from the more traditional:

> And the LORD God said, "It is not good that the man should be alone; I will make him an help meet for him." And out of the ground the LORD God formed every beast of the field, and every fowl of the air; and brought them unto Adam… [King James, clarifying punctuation added]

to:

> The LORD God said, "It is not good for the man to be alone. I will make a helper suitable for him." Now the LORD God *had* formed out of the ground all the wild animals and all the birds in the sky. He brought them to the man… [New International Version, emphasis added].

The change is defended on the grounds that the original Hebrew may be understood this way. However, claiming that the original *may* be interpreted this way is not the same as demonstrating that this is the correct interpretation. For one thing, the New International translators themselves have to admit that the same form of the Hebrew can also be understood as a simple past tense, for – as biblical scholar Hector Avalos points out – that is how they translate it elsewhere. Genesis 2:7, for example, is rendered as "the Lord God formed the man from the dust of the living ground…" (not "*had* formed").[26] But what's worse is that it really doesn't seem their way of interpreting the above passage can be correct. God's stating "I will make a helper suitable for him," after all, makes little sense if the animals were already around. This solution, then, does not appear entirely adequate.

Another possible explanation of the contradiction between chapters one and two is that the Adam and Eve story is not intended as a chronological account at all; rather, it is meant to provide further details regarding the origin of human beings, and perhaps also to convey our relative importance over the rest of creation. The emphasis in Genesis 2, it is claimed, is not on when the animals and other non-human things were created, but instead on their relationship to man. As inerrantists Norman Geisler and Thomas Howe put it in *The Big Book of Bible Difficulties*, "The focus in chapter 2 is on the *naming* of the animals, not on *creating* them."[27] Similarly, in his *Encyclopedia of Bible Difficulties*, Gleason Archer argues that Genesis 2 "was never intended to be a creation account," but "develops in detail one important feature that has already been mentioned [in Genesis 1]: the creation of man."[28] Unfortunately, these explanations ignore the simple fact that the Adam and Eve story does include its own timeline: like chapter one, it too is clearly arranged as a sequence of events. And the fact remains that the sequence is different in each case. The natural way to interpret the passage about the animals in chapter two is as an event that follows the appearance of Adam. Is there any doubt that if Genesis 2 was the only creation account, every true believer would claim man was created first?

There is another, more fundamental, difficulty involved in all attempts to resolve the contradictions: the previously mentioned problem of unclarity. God, being omniscient, would have known that the two distinct versions as written would result in confusion and lead to doubts regarding the accuracy of the scriptures. He might even predict that one day atheists would write books such as this one. It seems, then, that if these creation stories really were God's work, they would have been made clearer in the first place. The fact that the issue of consistency can be raised at all is evidence that the Bible is not the word of God.

As to the real reason for the discrepancies, the simple fact is that the first two chapters of Genesis come from two different sources, representing two distinct traditions. The six day creation story, which makes up the first chapter,* is from what is known as the *Priestly source*, a work written during or after the period of Babylonian captivity (and which contains much that the Israelites got from the Babylonians, including the tale of the Flood). In it, God is a spirit who creates the world directly, simply by uttering commands, such as "Let there be light." The Adam and Eve story, on the other hand, is from the so-called *Yahwist source*, which is believed to be several hundred years older. In this earlier account, God is an anthropomorphic deity who walks around the Garden of Eden, creates the first man by molding him out of dirt, and makes use of a rib in order to manufacture Eve. The writers of these respective myths were working with very different concepts. It should not be surprising that the stories they tell are also very different.

Similar difficulties – and often more serious ones – plague attempts to resolve other contradictions in scripture. We will consider some of these in the next

---

* And a bit of the second chapter, for it actually ends with Genesis 2:3. The reason for this is that the division into chapters was not in the original writings, but came much later.

chapter, when we examine the New Testament in some detail. For now, it is sufficient to point out that such things as the different accounts of Jesus's post-resurrection appearances, the question whether salvation is by faith alone or faith and good works (or even faith *or* good works), and many, many other examples, show that the various writers involved were often unaware of, had forgotten, or simply disagreed with what others had said. When the Bible is approached objectively, it can be seen for what it really is: a collection of stories produced by very fallible, very human authors – and not the work of an omniscient God.

SCIENTIFIC ERRORS AND WHAT THEY REVEAL

The Bible is also in contradiction with reality. Now, it is true that some alleged factual mistakes can be explained, at least up to a point, as mistranslations or misinterpretations. I say "up to a point" because in certain cases there is still an underlying problem. Consider, for instance, the fact that the Bible calls the bat a bird.[29] God should know that bats are mammals; after all, he's the one who created them! There is, however, a pretty reasonable explanation for this apparent howler. The biblical writers used the term translated as "bird" to refer to any flying animal larger than an insect; the modern classification of animals into such classes as birds and mammals did not exist at the time. Hence, one might say there is no genuine error here. Nevertheless, there is still something puzzling. Animals in the Bible are classified into three principal groups: aquatic, terrestrial, and aerial. Now, this is a rather simplistic taxonomy. Bats have a lot more in common with elephants and dolphins than they have with owls and butterflies. It is understandable for ancient people to have grouped animals in this way, of course, and it might even be argued that it would make sense for God to communicate with such people using these rather basic concepts. That is why the bat is grouped with the birds and why the "great fish" that swallowed Jonah was almost certainly a whale. But how do we explain God himself adhering to this classification scheme? Genesis describes the creation of animals in stages, aquatic and aerial animals on one day, terrestrial ones on the next. Why would God regard a property like flight to be of such paramount importance? Are we to suppose that God created bats at the same time as most birds, but only got around to such creatures as the ostrich and the kiwi when he created land mammals? Of course the believer may hold that the creation story is a myth intended to convey something other than an accurate depiction of the origin of the universe. For example, it may simply be a way for God to express to human beings some idea of his great power. But that does not make the presence of its nonsensical details any easier to understand. It is obvious that such details could have been omitted without detracting from the main point being made. If, on the other hand, we take Genesis to be the work of pre-scientific human beings, the mystery vanishes.

There is a more general sort of scientific error found throughout scripture. Its overall view of the universe is primitive and anthropocentric. The sky, for instance, is regarded as a firmament – a solid roof – separating waters above it from waters below (Genesis 1:6-8, Proverbs 8:27-28); the sun is thought to travel around us and to be much smaller than the earth (Joshua 10:12-13); the stars are described as relatively small objects that can fall to the ground (Mark 13:25, Revelation 8:10); the earth is thought to be stationary and firmly set on a foundation (Psalm

104:5 and many other passages); and of course our planet is also assumed to be flat, as for example when Jesus sees all of the world from the top of a very tall mountain (Matthew 4:8), or when God is said to have "spread out the earth" (Isaiah 44:24).

As one might expect, these errors are denied by many believers. Consider the flat earth question. Not only do many deny that the Bible suggests such a thing, some argue that it actually implies the opposite. It is even common for believers to contend that there is proof of divine inspiration here: no human being at the time would have known the true shape of our planet, it is said, so if the Bible claims that we live on a round world, it must in fact be the word of God.

The strongest evidence for a spherical earth in scripture is found in Isaiah 40:22, which refers to the "circle of the earth":

> It is he that sitteth upon the circle of the earth, and the inhabitants thereof are as grasshoppers; that stretcheth out the heavens as a curtain, and spreadeth them out as a tent to dwell in...

Note however that the skies are described as a "tent" over this circle. What this suggests, therefore, is not a sphere, but something in the shape of a disc – a not unnatural idea for ancient people who contemplated the apparent shape of the sky and of the horizon. Similarly, in Proverbs 8:27-29, which also mentions a circular shape, we have:

> ...when he drew a circle on the face of the deep, when he made firm the skies above... when he assigned to the sea its limit, so

that the waters might not transgress his command... [NRSV]

Not only is the sky once again above this circle, but the sea has limits, apparently to prevent the water from falling off. This is similar to a theory proposed by some flat-earthers of more recent times. Wilbur Voliva, a biblical literalist who until the 1940's was the leader of a cult of about six thousand in the small town of Zion, Illinois, held that the earth is a disc with the North Pole at its center and Antarctica as a wall of ice around the edges. This wall of course prevented ships from falling into Hades below.[30] Had the writers of scripture been familiar with the polar regions, they would most likely have reached similar conclusions.

A different explanation sometimes offered for the errors found in scripture – one that at least admits it contains actual falsehoods – is based on a theory known as divine accommodation. The idea is that God reveals truths to human beings piecemeal, as we develop to the point where we are ready to accept them. If God were to inform the ancients about such facts as the big bang, evolution, or the true shape of our planet, they would merely become confused, and would reject his word. Thus, God had to suggest a view of things more appropriate to their level of understanding.

Now, one problem with this theory is that there were rough contemporaries who knew that the earth was round. Pythagoras, in the sixth century BCE, is reported to have believed it, and by the next century it had become the common view among Greek philosophers. Aristotle provided all of the basic arguments available to earthbound observers in support of the idea, and Plato even imagined how our world would resemble a multicolored ball if seen from a great distance.[31] It seems reasonable, then, that at least by Jesus's time the writers of scripture could have been informed of the facts. Moreover, there does not appear to be any justification along these lines for such notions as that the sky was a dome with water above it, that the stars were so small they might fall to the ground, or that plants were created before the sun and the moon. Was it really necessary for God to mislead humanity with so many absurd claims?

The most significant thing about biblical cosmology is not that it is wrong, but that it is wrong in a not-at-all-unexpected kind of way. The scriptures describe essentially what the universe might have been like had it been created by a deity for the sake of mankind. That is, if human beings are the reason behind creation, as the Bible implies, then the universe should be fairly small, the earth might very well be at its center, and we should have been here almost from the beginning. Celestial objects most likely would not be other worlds – for what would be the point of uninhabited planets? The earth, being in a different category from the heavenly bodies, might very well be unlike them, and thus be a flat disc, firmly set on a fixed foundation. It makes little sense, by contrast, for God to create a mostly empty, unimaginably vast cosmos as our home, and then wait close to fourteen billion years before placing humans in it by the apparently random and rather wasteful process of evolution. And the vastness, both in space and in time, is nothing less than astounding.

In *The Dragons of Eden*, Carl Sagan uses a "cosmic calendar" to represent the history of the universe, from the big bang to the present moment, as a single year. On this scale, the first members of our species appear on December 31 around 11:53 p.m., and recorded history takes up less than the last twelve seconds before midnight.* The universe has been around approximately seventy thousand times as long as humans have, and about two million seven-hundred and fifty-thousand times as long as all of recorded history. If the biblical view is correct, what was the point of all those past eons of time? And the *size* of the universe is even harder to explain if everything was put here for our benefit. Even the solar system is much larger than seems necessary. Travelling at 1000 km/h (approximately 620 mph), it would take over seventeen years to reach the sun, and close to seven hundred years to reach Pluto. To get to the nearest star would take considerably longer: more than four-and-a-half million years, in fact. (Four-and-a-half million years ago, the australopithecines had yet to appear.) And to cross the Milky Way galaxy one would need over one hundred *billion* years, several times the current age of the universe. But that is still only a very tiny fraction of the totality of existence, for the observable universe contains at least one hundred billion galaxies, each containing countless stars. Nor is that necessarily all: there are reasons to believe that what we can see is but one very tiny portion of an ensemble of worlds many trillions of times larger, and possibly infinitely old. What is the purpose of it all?

Given the biblical view of man's place in creation, the actual scale of the universe, both temporally and spatially, becomes something of a mystery. God might have created such a universe, but it is not at all what one would have expected. A relatively small, young, earth-centered cosmos would appear to be much more in order. Above, I

---

* Sagan doesn't mention when *Homo sapiens* arrived on the scene, but rather when the first members of our genus did so; thus he gives 10:30 p.m. on Dec. 31 as the time of the first humans.

mentioned flat-earther Wilbur Voliva. One of his arguments concerned the distance and size of the sun, which he maintained to be 32 miles in diameter and at most 3000 miles away: "It stands to reason it must be so," he said. "God made the sun to light the earth, and therefore must have placed it close to the task it was designed to do."[32] This may be ridiculous, but the fact is that it's much more in line with the biblical view of things than is reality. That the universe is not at all like what is assumed in scripture is therefore evidence that the Bible is the work of pre-scientific human beings, and nothing more.

THE MORALITY OF THE OLD TESTAMENT

As great as all of the above problems are, an even more serious challenge for the believer concerns the rather obvious discrepancy between God's supposed goodness and the disturbing actions he performs and commands throughout much of the Old Testament. Let us initially concentrate on just three main examples of this (though some additional ones will be briefly mentioned later on). Whether these examples report actual events or not is irrelevant. Even if the believer claims that they are mere tales, the fact remains that they are meant to convey, or at least that they assume, certain moral principles, and the question is whether these principles are good ones.

I'll begin with the following inspiring story told about the prophet Elisha, one of the most important of all prophets in the Good Book:

> And he went up from thence unto Beth-el: and as he was going up... there came forth little children out of the city and mocked

him, and said unto him, "Go up, thou bald head; go up, thou bald head." And he turned back, and looked on them, and cursed them in the name of the LORD. And there came forth two she bears out of the wood, and tare forty and two of them.[33]

The punishment for these misbehaving kids was to at least be mauled by bears. It follows that if God is morally perfect, it must be right to brutally injure children for the offense of mocking a man's receding hair line. And that's if we interpret the passage charitably: there is a strong suggestion that the children were in fact slaughtered.

The second example I'll use concerns the commandment (with which Jesus apparently disagreed)[34] forbidding all work on the Sabbath:

And while the children of Israel were in the wilderness, they found a man that gathered sticks upon the sabbath day. And they that found him gathering sticks brought him unto Moses and Aaron, and unto all the congregation. And they put him in ward, because it was not [clear] what should be done to him. And the LORD said unto Moses, "The man shall be surely put to death: all the congregation shall stone him with stones [outside] the camp." And all the congregation brought him [outside] the camp, and stoned him with stones, and he died; as the LORD commanded Moses.[35]

This man's crime was gathering sticks on a Saturday, probably fire wood for cooking or for warmth. If any court today sentenced someone to death for anything so inconsequential it would be condemned by the majority of the world, and rightly so.

My final example is about what God instructs the Israelites to do with the inhabitants of conquered lands:

> But of the cities of these people, which the LORD thy God doth give thee for an inheritance, thou shalt save alive nothing that breatheth: But thou shalt utterly destroy them; namely, the Hittites, and the Amorites, the Canaanites, and the Perizzites, the Hivites, and the Jebusites; as the LORD thy God hath commanded thee: That they teach you not to do after all their abominations, which they have done unto their gods...[36]

The Israelites proceed to slaughter everyone, including youngsters and infants (and even animals, for they also breathe), in the overpowered cities. That people today defend such actions because they were supposedly commanded by God is one of the most disturbing aspects of religion. Murdering all adult inhabitants in order to prevent their religious beliefs from spreading is despicable enough. But killing even the small children is truly monstrous, and as great an evil as has ever been perpetrated by anyone. The slaughter of the innocents allegedly ordered by King Herod is viewed with horror by Christians – as of course it should be: had it been an actual historical event, it would have been the single worst act of a very evil tyrant. And yet here is their loving God, the being whom they worship as morally perfect, ordering essentially the same thing. If the children of these conquered lands had been spared and brought up by the Israelites, they would not have brought with them any religious views. It seems, then, that they could have been adopted instead of murdered. (And if the theist objects that perhaps the Israelites would not have the resources with which to take care of all these additional individuals, I will remind him that he believes in a God who on another occasion provided his people with manna from heaven.)

The above is not by any means the only instance of God-commanded mass killings in the Good Book. There are unfortunately numerous similar examples. In Exodus 32, Moses, on God's orders, has three thousand of his own people slaughtered for the crime of worshipping a golden calf. Those under his command were told to kill their friends, neighbors, even members of their own families. Moses then praises his assassins by telling them they brought a blessing on themselves that day, "each one at the cost of a son or a brother."[37] Or consider the conquest of the Midianites. On that occasion, God told his people to "kill every male among the little ones, and kill every woman that hath known man by lying with him. But all the women children, that have not known a man by lying with him, keep alive for yourselves."[38] Comparable atrocities are found repeatedly in such books as Deuteronomy and Joshua. Even so, none of these qualifies as the most disturbing thing contained within the pages of the Bible. That distinction arguably goes to Hosea 13:16, which describes how God will soon punish the Israelites in Samaria for worshipping the wrong deities. Because they have "rebelled against" their God, it says, "their infants shall be dashed in pieces, and their pregnant women shall be ripped open." As New Testament scholar Bart Ehrman observed, this "is not the kind, loving, caring, forgiving God" normally taught in Sunday schools.[39]

What can the believer say about such horrible things? We will consider five different explanations that have been offered. Some of these are general, others are aimed at specific difficulties; some concentrate on what God commanded the Israelites to do on given occasions, others deal specifically with Old Testament laws. The problem, as we'll see, is that none of them work.

(1) The explanation that appears to be the most popular with the average believer states that, by dying on the cross, Jesus "fulfilled" the Old Testament law, and by doing so freed us from having to obey the former rules that had been laid down by God. Never mind that Jesus himself said "I have not come to abolish the law or the prophets" and that "whoever breaks one of the least of these commandments... will be called least in the kingdom of heaven."[40] According to proponents of this view, the original covenant has in fact been repealed. That is why Paul said that "we are discharged from the law... so that we are slaves not under the old written code but in the new life of the Spirit."[41] It follows that we no longer have to stone people to death for working on Saturday, which is certainly welcome news (we probably wouldn't be able to find enough rocks with which to do the job). Unfortunately, however, this is no answer to the problem – and not just because Paul and those who agree with him contradict Jesus. First of all, it still follows that it would have been right to stone people to death for all sorts of things back in Old Testament times. That the moral code has changed, even if true, does nothing to alter that fact. Second, and even worse, the claim that we are no longer bound by the old laws is not equivalent to the claim that they are no longer morally acceptable. It may no longer be *necessary* to follow them; but that by itself does not imply

that it would be *wrong* to do so. At the very least, then, more needs to be said.

(2) Our next proposal claims that in ancient times *circumstances* were different, and that this is what provides the rationale for the severe nature of the Old Testament laws. On this view, the old laws have been repealed because conditions have changed. Though this can be combined with the first solution, it is also an improvement over it. It at least explains why it no longer would be right to act in accordance with the ancient codes. The problem for the proponent of this idea, however, is to find plausible reasons for the change. What fact about the world during biblical times could possibly have made the slaughter of innocents justified? Were things really that different back then? The answer, according to some, is found in the concept of divine accommodation, which the reader may remember from the previous section. The ancient laws were barbaric because the people were barbaric, and could not have been expected to comply with higher ideals. God therefore gave us his laws not all at once, but in an incremental fashion, as we became psychologically capable of accepting them. Paul Copan, a well-known religious philosopher, put it this way: "God begins with an ancient people who have imbibed dehumanizing customs and social structures from their ancient Near Eastern context. Yet Yahweh desires to treat them as morally responsible agents who, it is hoped, *gradually* come to discover a better way; he does this rather than risk their repudiating a loftier ethic – a moral overhaul – that they cannot even understand and for which they are not culturally or morally prepared."[42] In other words, it would not have done any good for God to ask them to obey the Golden Rule – they would simply have laughed at such a noble

principle. Instead, he had to give them laws that they might actually follow. (True, the command to love one's neighbor as oneself is already found in Leviticus, but never mind that!)

In order for this argument to work, it must be the case that God's laws were at least an improvement over the standard of the day, a step up along the path that presumably culminated with the Sermon on the Mount. And that is exactly what Copan argues. He claims that the laws of Moses showed relative "restraint" when contrasted with other ancient edicts. As one example of a harsh set of laws, he mentions Hammurabi's Code, which he tells us included such penalties as that of having anyone accused of a crime "being dragged around a field by cattle."[43] Moses's law, by comparison, included the following punishments: a son who is disobedient to his mother or father shall be stoned to death (Deuteronomy 21:18-21); a woman who is not a virgin at the time of her wedding shall be stoned by the men of the city in front of her father's house (Deuteronomy 22:20-21); and, of course, anyone who tries to convince you to worship a different God, *even if she is your mother, your spouse or your own child*, must similarly be punished: "thou shalt surely kill him; thine hand shall be first upon him to put him to death..." (Deuteronomy 13:6-9). Now, I have little doubt that other ancient legal codes contained equally harsh measures. But for Copan to mention being dragged by cattle as an example of something worse than anything in the Bible is simply incomprehensible. At any rate, Mosaic Law was certainly not superior in any important respect to others in the ancient Middle East.

As to the central point of the argument – which is that God could not have expected people back then to follow a higher moral standard and therefore had to resort to a compromise – it fails on at least two counts. First, it is not any easier to uphold a law which prescribes death for relatively minor offences than one that does not. What would have been so hard for the Israelites to understand about punishing disobedient children in a somewhat less extreme manner? According to Copan's way of looking at things, they were expected to adhere to the law when it came to such things as performing circumcisions and staying away from shellfish, but they could not possibly be expected to restrain themselves from killing their own unruly kids. That is absurd. God was so demanding about so many specific issues – including even prohibiting his people from wearing clothing made of blended materials[44] – but he saw no need to prevent unjustified killing?

The second and more serious reason why this argument does not succeed is that it fails to explain the existence of the harsh laws in the first place. Even if for some reason we grant that the people could not follow a more enlightened ethic, it does not follow that God had to command them to do that which is immoral. You don't make people *less* barbaric by ordering them to stone others to death. What would have happened, say, if God had simply *not* prohibited work on the Sabbath? It seems at the very least that the man who picked up the sticks would have been spared. This attempt at defending the Old Testament therefore fails as well.

(3) Maybe the next explanation will fare better. The suggestion is that in certain cases the Bible has been mistranslated. This is one claim often made regarding the Elisha episode, the first of the events mentioned above. According to some apologists, the bears did not in fact attack little children, but young men. The Hebrew words used for "little" and "boys," they argue, are also used for "young" and "lads" respectively. And if these individuals

were actually a gang of young ruffians openly mocking Elisha because he was God's prophet, the claim goes, then they deserved to be mauled by wild animals.

I'll leave aside the question whether or not there is reason to accept this new interpretation of the story, and whether in that case the young men deserved their punishment. Even if both of those are granted, there is a catch. An all-seeing God would have known that the words used by his divinely-inspired writer would likely get mistranslated, with the result that most people reading the book nowadays end up with the wrong impression. Instead of learning the actual story, we are led to believe that God mauls little children to death for misbehaving. This could easily have been avoided if the original passage had been written down in greater detail. What we have here, therefore, is at best another instance of the problem of unclarity. And so, once again, the apologist's argument does not work.

(4) The next explanation of the biblical atrocities is one that Copan mentions as well, though many others have made the same point. The problem as they see it is that the critic of the Bible is appealing to a moral standard that applies to human beings. But according to defenders of this view, God is not to be judged by such standards. God, after all, is the creator, and since he gave us life, he has the right to take it away. To quote Copan once more: "If God is the author of life – the cosmic authority – he is not obligated to give us seventy to eighty years of life... God can take Canaanite lives indirectly through Israel's armies – or directly, as with Sodom..."[45] In fact, an argument along these lines appears to be all but necessary if one is going to justify the most extensive atrocity in the Old Testament, the Flood. I have not mentioned that one until now because it is so familiar that people usually don't give

it a second thought. As a result, it might not seem as terrible at first as some of the other cruelties described above. But imagine what is supposed to have happened: God killed everyone on earth with the exception of eight people and a number of animals. Countless infants and small children were drowned on purpose – a horrible way to die – by the infinitely merciful Lord. And yet he is regarded as morally perfect. People *must* be judging him by a different standard!

The idea, then, is that as the one who created us, God is perfectly within his rights if he wishes to destroy us. The Lord giveth and the Lord taketh away. But is that right? Suppose you suddenly found yourself with the power to create life. You create an entire civilization of miniature beings who think of you as their god. You can see from observing them through a microscope that they are every bit as complex as humans, caring for their loved ones, planning for the future, and so on. Does it follow *from the mere fact that you created them* that it would be acceptable for you to now destroy them? I hope you agree that the answer is no. It would be nothing less than genocide. As soon as such creatures are created, it becomes wrong to kill them. Likewise, even if God made us, the fact is that we are here, sentient beings who care about others, who have hopes and dreams, and who are not deserving of death and suffering. It would be no more morally acceptable for God to kill us than for anyone else to do so. It makes no difference who performs the act: the end result would be the same.

(5) At this point, the believer might object that if God kills, he must have a good reason for doing so. Copan says as much, claiming God may take human life for "morally sufficient reasons."[46] But this changes the argument. Copan conflates this idea with the previous one, but now it

no longer is the case that God has the right to kill us because he is our creator; rather, his right derives from there being a *moral justification* for killing. What we have here, then, is yet another possible reason for the apparently immoral events found in the Bible. According to this view, the troubling episodes in the Old Testament are not what they at first appear to be, for they all have underlying reasons, even if we cannot always see what they are. We may simply not know, or not have thought about, all of the details. In many cases, we may simply be failing to keep the big picture in mind. What we have to do is take all of the facts into consideration.

Thus, one possible reply with regards to the annihilation of conquered tribes is simply to claim that it was fully justified by the terrible behavior of the people in question. Their "degenerate idolatry and moral depravity,"[47] according to some apologists, had to be entirely wiped out from the land. Geisler and Howe, in their work on Bible difficulties, remind readers that the Midianites, for one, had "corrupted God's people by leading them into idolatry at Baal-Peor so that 24,000 Israelites died in the plague."[48] Similarly, they say, it was "necessary to completely exterminate any trace of the city [of Jericho] and its people. If anything had remained, except that which was taken into the treasure house of the Lord, there would have always been the threat of heathen influence to pull the people away from the pure worship of the Lord."[49] Of course the plague that supposedly occurred as a result of idolatry was presumably sent by Yahweh, who after all is, by his own admission, an angry and jealous God. Moreover, it's somewhat debatable whether worshipping other gods merits being massacred and having even your small children put to death. (It is also interesting that in the almost complete destruction of

Jericho an exception was made of the silver and gold, so that it could be taken into "the treasure house of the Lord"; religion, it seems, never changes.)

Now, it is true that there were many behaviors among these conquered peoples which were genuinely bad. They apparently engaged in child sacrifice, for example. But it should be pointed out, first, that to put a stop to child sacrifice by killing everyone involved *including the children* does not seem entirely sensible; and second, that early on in their history, the Israelites seem to have performed such sacrifices as well. It was sadly an all-too-common practice, and, as will be shown in the next chapter, there is biblical evidence that God's chosen people were no different from other tribes in this respect. But if that is true, then the fact that other tribes engaged in this practice could not be the reason why God commanded their annihilation.

There is another problem with this attempted solution to the savagery promoted in the Bible. If worshipping other gods is regarded by Yahweh as such a great evil, why is the destruction of rival religious traditions no longer commanded by him today? What explains the change? One answer, offered by Gleason Archer, is that Christians don't have to behave as the ancient Israelites did because, being empowered by the Holy Spirit within them, they "possess resources for resisting the corrupting influence of unconverted worldlings," and are thus "able to lead [their] lives in the midst of a corrupt and degenerate non-Christian culture (whether in the Roman Empire or in modern secularized Europe or America) and still keep true to God." It is for this reason that they "have no occasion as ambassadors for Christ to resort to physical weapons to protect [their] faith..."[50] What Archer is maintaining here, in other words, is that if it were not for the empowering influence of the Holy Spirit, Christians *would* be justified in killing non-Christians! They don't have to, but only because they have an inner strength that allows them to remain uncontaminated by the evil secularism and pagan religious practices that surround them. Such a view, however, is not only highly disturbing; it also fails to explain why the ancients couldn't likewise have been given this kind of inner strength.

There are other ways to maintain that the Israelites' behavior toward the conquered tribes was justified. The widely-respected Christian philosopher William Lane Craig, for instance, argues that in fact there was nothing wrong with the extermination of innocent children – for what we are forgetting, according to Craig, is the afterlife: "if we believe, as I do, that God's grace is extended to those who die in infancy or as small children, the death of these children was actually their salvation… Therefore, God does these children no wrong in taking their lives."[51] In other words, murdering kids can be good! It's a way to ensure that they end up in heaven. Geisler and Howe agree; they even call this annihilation "an act of God's mercy"[52] toward these children. The view that God was doing them a favor is also defended by Paul Copan[53] and several other fundamentalist apologists. I wonder how many decent, church-going Christians realize that such despicable claims are made in defense of their beliefs. These apologists ignore the fear, the pain, and the horror experienced by the small children as they watched their families being brutally slaughtered by the swords and spears of ruthless soldiers, before being massacred themselves. If that is not wrong, what is? Does anyone who has the slightest shred of human decency really think otherwise? And furthermore, as to this being the children's salvation – the implication here being that they were otherwise hell-bound – that is an attempt to justify one evil by the introduction of an even greater one. There wouldn't be a hell, after all, if God didn't create one. That, however, is a topic for the next chapter.

Every one of the religious arguments we have looked at is flawed. But there is, of course, a simple way to account for all of the biblical atrocities. Much of the Old Testament was composed by people whose moral views were very different from our own; people who, by our standards, were little more than primitive barbarians. Their moral principles were designed to justify, among other things, their own aggressive acts of war. It should come as no surprise, then, that the ideas they put in their God's mouth are no longer regarded as acceptable. Morality has improved since their time. It has moved on.

And you *shouldn't* thank God for that.

3

JESUS OF NAZARETH

...the day will come when the mystical generation of Jesus, by the Supreme Being as His Father in the womb of a virgin, will be classed with the fable of the generation of Minerva in the brain of Jupiter.

– Thomas Jefferson, letter to John Adams

For many, the proof that Christianity is the "one true religion" is found in the events that supposedly took place two thousand years ago in Palestine, and in particular the resurrection of Jesus of Nazareth. It is because of these alleged historical underpinnings that many hold Christianity to be in a separate category from the world's other great religions. Other faiths either have no basis in reality, or at best are based on fact mixed with legend. Christianity alone, it is said, is firmly grounded on eyewitness accounts of actual occurrences. Each gospel was reportedly written by an individual who had first-hand, or at least second-hand, knowledge of the events described. That, at any rate, is the traditional story. And since Jesus performed many miracles and conquered even death itself, he must have been who he claimed to be. Hence, nonbelievers are, as St. Paul said, without excuse.

Or are they? I believe that anyone who investigates these claims with an open mind will see that they are completely unjustified. Christianity is no more supported by evidence than is any other religion – which is to say that it is not supported by evidence at all. It is undeniable that its stories have some basis in fact, of course. There almost certainly was a real person named Jesus who lived during the first century, had a small group of followers, and was crucified by the Roman authorities. Some of his sayings were preserved by these followers and eventually written down, along with some of the most important events in his life – though the gospels were composed somewhat later, by people who probably never met him. Aside from that, very little is known with any kind of certainty. The majority of what Christians believe about Jesus is pure legend. Moreover, that this is the case is something we can see by examining the written record alone. So let's turn to that.

We'll begin by asking whether the New Testament writings concerning the life of Jesus and of his disciples can be trusted.

THE EVIDENCE

It is often claimed that the New Testament writings are at least as well-supported as other historical documents of the era – documents on which historians base their knowledge of the Roman and Greek worlds, among other things. However, even if that were the case it would hardly be sufficient. I say this because the events described in the gospels and the book of Acts are highly unusual. In addition to the resurrection, they include such things as a storm ending on command, the curing of blindness with saliva, a transfer of demons from a human being into some unfortunate pigs, and a small number of fish multiplying – and not in the usual fashion – into a great number of fish. But as Carl Sagan used to say, "extraordinary claims require extraordinary evidence." If you hear a report that there's been an accident on the highway, you don't ordinarily need additional corroboration to accept it as true. If, on the other hand, the report is that the accident was the result of a flying saucer landing in the middle of the road, you might want to look into it a bit further. The evidence for the stories found in the New Testament must therefore be of an extremely high caliber. But as it turns out, that's not the case – not even close. The writings concerning Jesus are in fact riddled with problems.

Many of the inconsistencies, anomalies, and other questionable statements in the New Testament are well known. Judas died by hanging himself after handing back his reward for betraying Jesus, but nevertheless also managed to purchase a field with the money – a field in which he then died by falling in such a way that "all his bowels gushed out."[54] The last supper took place either on the day of the Passover or one day before, depending on which gospel one consults. The time of the crucifixion varies from one account to another. And similar discrepancies are found in the genealogy of Jesus, his last words on the cross, the discovery of the empty tomb, the post-resurrection appearances, and numerous other matters – leading even C. S. Lewis to conclude that not everything in the New Testament is literally true. Now, all of these things have been cited countless times by skeptics, and one might therefore think it unnecessary to bring them up yet again. Nevertheless, some people who should know better are persuaded by the biblical accounts. Douglas Wilson, for instance, a knowledgeable pastor who wrote replies to several of the new atheist books (and who later debated Christopher Hitchens on the documentary film *Collision*), argues that the gospel writers could not have altered "the known facts" regarding Christ's life without being exposed as frauds by the critics of the new religion.[55]

One of the "facts" that Wilson appeals to is the story of Christ's birth, which he emphasizes would have been "a hard event to stage."[56] And yet what is really evident from the two birth narratives contained in the Bible is that the actual events surrounding the nativity – whatever they are – are not found there. For one thing, the narratives have very little in common with one another. About the only thing they share is the (almost certainly false) claim that Jesus was born in Bethlehem. Everything else related to this supposedly momentous occasion remains – as a brief outline of each story shows – extremely unclear.

According to Matthew's account, following the visit by the wise men, Joseph and his family ran away to Egypt to escape Herod's attempt to kill Jesus, and it was only upon returning to the Holy Land, after Herod's death, that they decided to settle in Nazareth. For, "when [Joseph] heard that Archelaus was ruling over Judea in place of his father Herod, he was afraid to go there. And after being warned in a dream, he went away to the district of Galilee. There he made his home in a town called Nazareth..."[57] This is the first time Nazareth is mentioned in the gospel, and the implication is clear that it is not where the family was originally from. Luke's story, on the other hand, *begins* in Nazareth: it is there that Mary learns from the angel

Gabriel that she will bear the son of God. Later, the Roman emperor orders a census to be taken of the whole empire and (strangely enough) Joseph has to go to Bethlehem to be registered for it, because that was the city of his ancestor David. Mary goes along with him and while there, of course, she gives birth to Jesus in the famous manger scene. Afterwards, the family "returned into Galilee, to their *own city* Nazareth."[58] According to Luke, then, Joseph and Mary were Nazarenes all along. Moreover, no mention is made of a temporary exile in Egypt.

These accounts are not only utterly inconsistent with one another, they in addition have all the earmarks of being fabricated. The gospel of Matthew, written primarily for a Jewish audience, is intent on drawing parallels between Jesus and Moses. Both come "out of Egypt"[59] and both narrowly escape being killed in infancy, Moses on the orders of the pharaoh and Jesus on the orders of Herod. As to Luke's story, it simply lacks credibility. It's not just that there is no record of such a census being taken by the Romans at the time. The more serious question is why in order to be counted someone would have to return to the city of one of their ancestors – and especially of an ancestor who lived a thousand years earlier! As Bart Ehrman pointedly asks regarding this episode, "If we had a new worldwide census today and each of us had to return to the towns of our ancestors a thousand years back – where would *you* go?"[60] What is patently clear, then, is that both Matthew and Luke have invented stories regarding Jesus's birth. And the reason for this seems plain enough: at the time there were already some raising the objection that the messiah had to be born in Bethlehem, and not Nazareth, due to the prophecy written in Micah 5:2. This prophecy would have created a problem for the early Christians if Jesus was indeed from the little Galilean town of Nazareth. In fact, John 7:41-43 records an instance of this very objection from some who had heard the supposed messiah speak. Both Matthew and Luke, then, had to tell the story in such a way so as to have the birth occur in the right place. And of course, contrary to what Pastor Wilson suggests, the events described did not have to be "staged." They were simply made up. We should keep in mind that Matthew and Luke probably wrote their tales between seventy and ninety-five years after Jesus's birth – and it's not as if there were records in those days that people could check.

Attempts by believers to smooth over the difficulties in the New Testament are, much like the ones we encountered in the previous chapter, hardly ever credible. Consider the fact that Jesus is described as being descended from King David via two very different genealogical lines: the one in Matthew is twenty-seven generations long and makes him a descendant of David's son Solomon; the one in Luke is forty-two generations long and makes him a descendant of another of David's sons, Nathan. How can one make sense of such a thing? The standard reply is that one of the lines traces Jesus's ancestry through his father's (that is, Joseph's) side of the family while the other does so through his mother's side – admittedly, a creative attempt to explain away the contradiction. Nevertheless, as a solution to the problem it is far from satisfactory. First, both lines end with Joseph, so that in addition to the above, the apologist has to say that Joseph is listed as a son in one list, but as a *son-in-law* in the other – in spite of the fact that he is specifically referred to as the son in both genealogies. Second, part of the genealogical line in Matthew is found in 1 Chronicles as well – but once again, with discrepancies between the two.[61] Matthew leaves several names out. (The reason he does this is so that he could claim there were exactly fourteen generations from Abraham to David, another fourteen from David to the Babylonian captivity, and again fourteen from the Babylonian captivity until Jesus – and what this in turn shows is that Matthew was not so much interested in reporting facts as he was in telling a story with deeper theological significance.)

Many of the contradictions in the gospels, such as the two already discussed, are likely a result of their having distinct sources. In other words, incompatible stories about the same fact or event were told by different early Christians, and it just so happens that more than one of them found its way into scripture. Now, it is of course to be expected that the writers in question might not get their stories straight when their writings were completely independent of one another, as in the above examples. To make matters worse, however, they sometimes changed the details even when they did have another gospel as a source – as was the case with Matthew and Luke. Both of them used Mark,[62] yet neither remained faithful to that earlier account. That they changed some of the details should not be too surprising, however. None of them had any idea these four particular works would one day end up in the Bible (and there were many other gospels that didn't make the cut). In addition, Luke specifically states, at the beginning of his work, that even though others have written about these matters, he has made a careful investigation, and is writing so that he can teach "the truth concerning" them – all of which suggests that, in his opinion, others had perhaps not been so diligent.[63] The gospel writers, then, made revisions to earlier reports. And though the variation in these cases is usually not quite as great as in the ones already discussed, it is still very significant. As an example, both Matthew and Luke make changes to Mark's description of the discovery of the empty tomb. (John, meanwhile – probably writing independently – tells the most dissimilar story of all.)

The number of women who find the tomb open, as almost everyone realizes, differs in all four gospels. John mentions only Mary Magdalene making the discovery, Matthew has two women, Mark three, and Luke states that there were several. Apologists insist that there is no problem here, for the claim that a given person was involved does not rule out there being other individuals present as well. The accounts are not contradictory, they argue, merely incomplete. Strictly speaking, this is correct; it's just not very convincing. John's version, in particular, clearly implies that Mary Magdalene was there all by herself. Similarly, Mark mentions a young man sitting inside the tomb, whereas Matthew has an angel who sits outside, Luke has two men standing inside, and John two angels sitting inside, followed by the reappearance of Jesus – this last detail a *very* interesting omission in three out of the four gospels! The question that should be asked is why such an important event – one regarded as absolutely crucial evidence – is presented in such an utterly incoherent and confusing way. This is the problem of unclarity all over again. And the explanation, obviously, is that the story changed over time.

In order to make the resurrection tale more plausible, Christian apologists often bring up two interesting points. One is that the apostles were willing to die for their beliefs – which they claim shows they were convinced that Jesus had been raised from the dead. The other is that the individuals who discovered the empty tomb, whoever they were exactly, were women. But women, they remind us, were not regarded as reliable witnesses in those days. Hence, if the story had been made up, the writers would have said that it was *men* who made the discovery. This, therefore, demonstrates that the resurrection must have happened, they say.

Let's take up the latter claim first. The discovery of the empty tomb by women is already present in the earliest gospel, that of Mark. But here the apologists' argument immediately runs into a problem, for (even though most Christians undoubtedly are unaware of this) the ending to Mark has been tampered with. In present day Bibles, the gospel ends with post-resurrection accounts that resemble those in Luke and John. However, it is very likely that in its original form the work concluded with verse 16:8, with the women who had found the empty tomb running away from it in terror and reporting what they saw to no one, "for they were afraid." The verses that follow 16:8 (of which there are two main versions, one long and one short) are rather different in style from the rest of the gospel, and are not included in the oldest surviving manuscripts. Moreover, as Ehrman points out, the transition at this point makes little sense: in verse 16:9, Mary Magdalene is introduced as if she hadn't been mentioned yet, even though she was referred to just a few lines back.[64] These verses are therefore almost without any doubt later additions.

Now, it is possible that Mark originally had a different ending which has been lost. There are at least two reasons for thinking that is not the case, however. First, as some biblical scholars have pointed out, an ending to Mark in which the disciples never learn about the resurrection (because the women keep silent) fits naturally into one of the themes of that gospel, namely, that Jesus was misunderstood by those around him. Throughout his account, Mark suggests that the disciples never fully understood who Jesus was. It could be that with the original ending, the author was telling the reader, in effect, that they *never did* find out.[65] And second, the post-resurrection appearances in Matthew and Luke are utterly dissimilar. In Matthew, an angel at the empty tomb tells Mary Magdalene and "the other Mary" that Jesus has already headed toward Galilee[66] (which is a region about one hundred kilometers north of Jerusalem). Soon after that, as the women are on their way to see the disciples, Jesus himself appears to them and says "go and tell my brothers to go to Galilee; there they will see me."[67] The disciples do as they're told, and when they encounter their former master there, some doubt it is really him – further indicating that this is the first time they are meeting Jesus after the crucifixion. Now contrast this with Luke's story. In that gospel, Jesus first appears to two of his followers on the road to Emmaus, a village near Jerusalem.[68] These two then return to the eleven to inform them of what had happened. Immediately after that, Jesus appears to all of them inside their hideout in Jerusalem, and afterwards accompanies them to Bethany (also nearby) where he is carried away to heaven.[69] If Mark included any details about events following the discovery of the empty tomb, and these were available to Matthew and Luke, the complete lack of agreement between the latter two gospels would be that much harder to explain. The inconsistencies here are even greater than those one finds in the discovery of the empty tomb. They are more akin to the differences between their nativity stories – differences that are the result of their not having the same source at all.

It seems likely, then, that Mark did end at verse 16:8. And this is the earliest surviving gospel, which suggests that this was the original version of the story. If the story as first told included accounts of the women telling the disciples what they had seen, it would have been very strange indeed for Mark to not only have left that out, but to specifically imply the opposite. But now here's the problem: if in the original version of this tale the women run away and tell no one, then there was no implication that their testimony was used to back up the claim that Jesus returned from the grave. Thus, the fact that women were regarded as unreliable is utterly beside the point. They were not portrayed as the source of the information found in the gospel. In fact, they are represented as acting in a manner entirely consistent with how women were expected to behave: running away in terror, too scared to tell anyone what they had witnessed. Whoever came up with this story certainly does not appear to have had a very high opinion of them.

Now, one might reasonably wonder how anyone knew what happened if the women did not report it. Christian philosopher William Lane Craig even concludes that the claim that they told no one must apply only to the *immediate* future. Eventually, they must have reported it to someone – "otherwise," Craig reasons, "Mark couldn't be telling the story about it!"[70] But this of course assumes that the incident actually occurred. If someone made the whole thing up, it is obvious how he could tell the story without anyone having talked! (And if Craig's point is that the story in Mark – whether fictional or not – logically implies that the women informed someone, then my reply is that that's not supported by the internal evidence: there is nothing in Mark to suggest that the author was that concerned with logical consistency.)

There is one other potential difficulty here: why did the author of this story choose women in the first place? But that, too, does not appear all that difficult to explain. As writer-historian Earl Doherty points out, the disciples had supposedly gone into hiding, and so it would be strange for them to visit the tomb without having a good reason to do so. (As a matter of fact, in both Mark and Matthew there is no indication that they came to check on it even *after* it was found empty, and there are good reasons for thinking that the one passage in Luke that mentions Peter doing so was a later addition.)[71] Moreover, the reason given for visiting the tomb was the anointing of the body, and that was the responsibility of women.[72] The hypothesis that someone invented this entire episode also finds support in Paul's description of the post-resurrection appearances. When he lists whom Jesus appeared to, Paul, writing earlier than any of the gospel authors, begins with Peter and then mentions the other apostles – yet he never says anything about the women who supposedly first saw the risen Christ.[73]

What about the idea that Jesus's followers were willing to give up their lives for him? Leaving aside how we even know what happened to most of these followers (for the evidence is not significantly better in this case than for the rest of the events related in the New Testament), the fact that they were willing to die for their faith, if true, proves nothing. Muslim extremists, as we are all too aware, are also willing to kill themselves, and yet no Christian regards this as proof that the Koran is the word of God. Religious zealots and political fanatics of all stripes are perfectly capable of sacrificing their lives for some cause. All this proves is that the followers of Jesus, if they acted similarly, were "true believers." And to be true believers, they would not have had to see Jesus come back to life.

So far, we have seen that the various stories told about Jesus conflict with one another. However, as with the Old Testament difficulties covered in the previous chapter, the problems in the New Testament are by no means limited to contradictions. There are many other clear indications that these writings cannot be trusted. Consider Jesus's failed prophecy regarding the end of the world. Speaking about what is now interpreted as the second coming (the arrival of the Son of Man in power and glory, accompanied by the darkening of the sun and the falling of stars from the heavens), he announced that "this generation shall not pass, till all these things be fulfilled"[74] and that "there be some standing here, which shall not taste of death, till they see the kingdom of God."[75] The obvious non-fulfillment of this prophecy has been an embarrassment to Christianity ever since, and even led to a myth about a "wandering Jew," a figure who was around in Jesus's time and is still with us today, awaiting his return.[76] A rather more plausible explanation is that Jesus was a failed apocalyptic preacher, fully expecting the end of the world to come during the lifetime of at least some of his followers. That he was mistaken demonstrates, of course, that he was not God.

We are also told, in the gospel of Matthew, that on the day of the crucifixion there was darkness from noon until three,[77] and that the "graves were opened; and many bodies of the saints which slept arose... and went into the holy city, and appeared unto many."[78] It is interesting that there is no non-biblical source confirming these astonishing events. One would think that daytime darkness and dead people coming out of their graves and walking around town would have been widely reported, yet no contemporary historian seems to have noticed, or so much as heard of, any of these things. Worse, the episode of the walking dead isn't described anywhere else in the Bible either – neither the other gospels nor Paul ever mention it – even though such an event would surely be known and would constitute strong evidence in favor of the new religion.

Every one of these issues is a serious problem, and there are many, many others – so many, in fact, that (one is tempted to say) the world itself might not be able to contain all of the books that could be written about them. The New Testament, then, is far from reliable as a historical document. It not only provides zero actual evidence for such events as the resurrection; in light of its internal inconsistencies and obvious legendary details, it in fact presents us with grounds for regarding many of its stories as pure fabrication. Clearly, Christianity is like any other ancient superstition. It is no more believable than the mythology of the Greeks or Romans.

For many, however, the greatest obstacle towards accepting the religion lies in Jesus's support of the doctrine of eternal damnation. This troubling aspect of Christianity is the subject of our next section.

WHAT THE HELL?

If you debate the question of God's existence often, it is nearly certain that sooner or later you will be asked, "What if you're wrong?" The threat of hell is alive and well. It is famously found in Pascal's Wager, the argument devised by the 17th-century scientist, mathematician, and gambling Christian Blaise Pascal: if you believe in God, there is a chance you will gain eternal bliss; if you do not, there is a chance you will suffer eternal damnation; the better bet, Pascal concludes, is to believe. But even those who have never heard of Pascal's Wager resort to this type of intimidation.

The notion that nonbelievers are condemned may be thought a strong point in favor of Christianity – what better reason than *that* to convert? – but is actually one of the principal reasons for rejecting it. For how could a perfectly good God create hell? Nothing in Christianity is as puzzling as the fact that the Almighty is regarded both as a supremely moral, loving, and merciful being, and as one who horribly tortures many of his creatures in the afterlife – and not just for a little while, but for an unimaginably agonizing eternity. The immorality of the Old Testament, as we've already seen, is terrible and disturbing. And yet it pales in comparison to the traditional concept of everlasting punishment. As the writer (and theist) Martin Gardner put it, "if Jesus did indeed teach such a damnable doctrine, it is the strongest possible reason for not believing him to have been God in human flesh."[79]

The descriptions provided in the New Testament make clear what the threat, at least, is. Hell is a "place of torment,"[80] the "everlasting fire, prepared for the devil and his angels,"[81] where "there will be wailing and gnashing of teeth,"[82] and where the damned will be "tormented with fire and brimstone in the presence of the holy angels, and in the presence of the Lamb... and they have no rest day nor night."[83] But why should anyone be condemned to such a fate? The traditional answer is that we are all sinners, and thus all deserving of being cast into the flames. However, because God is a loving and merciful being, he pardons those who accept Jesus as having died for their sins. Often, the Christian adds that God is merely allowing each of us to make his or her own decision. God respects our choices, they say. He offers us forgiveness as a gift, but he cannot force us to accept it. That is why those who do not acknowledge Jesus have no excuse.

There are two issues that need to be addressed here. One concerns the idea of salvation through belief in Jesus, and why that should be the determining factor. That is something we will consider in the last section, on nonbelief. The other is this notion that, because we are sinners, we are deserving of eternal suffering. It is only if such a punishment is in fact warranted that the existence of hell can be justified in the first place. But why think that anyone – much less every single one of us – deserves to be in agony for all eternity?

This unfortunate doctrine is often defended on the grounds that even the tiniest sin is a crime against God; and that, since God is infinitely good, any crime against him is infinitely bad. Justice, therefore, requires the strongest possible retribution. On such a view, it follows that if someone lived exactly as God wanted her to live throughout her entire life – not merely in her outward actions, but even in her thoughts – with the single exception that on one occasion she told a little white lie in order to protect someone's feelings, then, assuming that all lying is sinful, this person deserves to suffer for all eternity. (And if lying is not invariably a sin then of course one could substitute some other minor wrong in its place.) My reply to this is simple: the claim that every wrong merits infinite punishment is ridiculous. I reject it as morally perverse, and so does anyone who is not under the obligation to defend this religious dogma. It is not that I, or anyone else, can *prove* it is wrong. In fact, as will be argued in chapter five, ethics is not a matter of truth and falsehood. Morality is dependent on our desires, on what we *feel* is good or bad; hence there is no fact of the matter here that can be demonstrated one way or the other. Nevertheless, most people, including most Christians, feel the way I do about the appropriate punishment for a minor wrong, namely that it should likewise be minor, and in many cases even nonexistent. We do not judge every moral infraction, no matter how small, as infinitely evil. The only wrong that actually seems to merit such a designation is precisely the one under discussion here: that of intentionally causing an infinite amount of suffering. In our ordinary, everyday lives, we simply do not believe that every human being deserves to be tortured forever. Instead, we believe that when horrible things are done to people, a great wrong is committed – and Christians feel this way even when the people in question happen to be non-Christian. In other words, they feel this way even when the victims are among the damned.

It seems obvious that most people just haven't given that much thought to the doctrine of eternal damnation. They do not appear to be aware of its actual implications. But consider this: to accept the doctrine is to accept the notion that even our loved ones – even our children, at least once they are sufficiently mature to make their own moral decisions – are so bad, so terribly depraved, that they deserve to be burned alive. I doubt many of even the most devout Christians can believe such a thing. At least I hope they cannot! One could say much more about such a horrible idea, of course. For instance, does it really make sense to claim that a wrong perpetrated against someone who is perfectly good is, for that reason, infinitely bad? And if God is in fact perfectly good, shouldn't that imply a tiny bit more mercy on his part? (If his mercy is conditional on believing in the implausible story of Jesus, whereas the rest can – quite literally – go to hell, then it hardly seems to qualify.) But I think it is enough to point out, as I've already done, that the entire premise here is simply absurd.

In any case, the doctrine of eternal damnation is so disturbing that many believers either reinterpret it, or else reject it outright. Some maintain that, contrary to what the Bible clearly states, everyone will be saved. Some say that at the very least people will be given a second chance, after Jesus returns, so that only those who sincerely desire hell as their final destination end up there. (I've always wondered just who those individuals might be!) A third option is to claim that some are saved and granted eternal life, while the rest simply perish. Of course it's still an enormous injustice for the gift of paradise to be limited to those who happen to believe in Jesus, but this is at least an improvement, since it is better to be annihilated – to simply go out of existence – than it is to suffer for all time. And finally, a fourth view is that hell is nothing more than the absence of God. All that talk of fire and brimstone is figurative. Those who do not accept God's offer of salvation end up being separated from God in the afterlife. Once again, this idea tends to be associated with the claim that it is really up to us – that the choice is ours to make. God allows those who would rather be separated from him to end up that way. Now, for an atheist, this may not sound so bad. After all, in heaven one might encounter Jerry Falwell and Oral Roberts, whereas in hell one will presumably find such individuals as Abraham Lincoln, Albert Schweitzer, and Mahatma Gandhi – and atheists are more likely to enjoy socializing with the latter. As another one of its presumed residents, Mark Twain, put it, each place has its advantages: "heaven for climate, hell for company."[84] The Christian proponents of this fourth view, however, emphasize that to be separated from God is in fact a terrible fate – just not as bad as eternal fire.

Religious philosopher J. P. Moreland, in what I think qualifies as one of the most amusing arguments ever presented by a serious thinker, finds support for this separation view in the Bible itself: "hell is described as a place of utter darkness and yet there are flames, too. How can that be? Flames would light things up."[85] Therefore, he insists, the flames aren't really there; they are just a symbolic means of expressing how bad the place is. Of course, the flames might still be there provided it is the *darkness* that is symbolic, but never mind that. The essential difficulty with these alternative views about hell is that if one does not take the Bible at face value, then one cannot be sure what damnation is actually supposed to be like. And this once again raises the problem of unclarity. Let's assume that Moreland is right. It nevertheless remains the case that the majority of Christians have believed in the fire and brimstone view, and that millions suffered from fear of the afterlife as a result. Even worse, their mistaken beliefs contributed to the extreme measures undertaken with regards to heathens: better that they be burned at the stake, after all, than that they remain alive to potentially lead others astray. The decisions made by the inquisitors and witch burners were, however, made under a misconception – and if that is the case, the responsibility for that misconception lies almost entirely with God.

Many other criticisms can be raised against the Pascal Wager style of argument. For instance, one might point out that the question "what if you're wrong?" applies to everyone, including Christians. Muslims, after all, think that every non-Muslim is damned – and what if it is *they* who are right? (Christians, interestingly, don't seem to lose any sleep over that possibility.) But the most appropriate reply to such arguments, in my opinion, is to turn the tables around, as I've done here. It isn't just that this is not a good argument in support of faith; it's that it makes for a very strong case against it. The concept of hell, no matter how one looks at it, should be regarded as an embarrassment by all true believers.

THE ATONEMENT

Hell is one thing. To raise objections to the atonement, on the other hand, might seem particularly depraved. After all, in the minds of most Christians, Jesus's sacrifice, in addition to being the very symbol of Christianity, stands as the ultimate reason for loving and honoring him. The observation that "Jesus died for you" is often stated in a tone indicating that nonbelievers are inexcusably ungrateful. How could anyone fail to acknowledge that wonderful, utterly selfless, act? However, the question whether such an act, if it occurred, is praiseworthy must be kept separate from other issues surrounding it. And there are, in fact, several problems with the crucifixion.

In the first place, what was Jesus trying to accomplish, exactly, by dying on the cross? The atonement is so familiar that most people never really stop to consider it. The basic idea, of course, is that he died in order to forgive us. But the question remains how his death is supposed to achieve such a result. Whatever the precise explanation is (and several theories have been proposed), it involves an innocent individual suffering instead of those who are guilty. But can such a thing ever be warranted? It seems it cannot. Consider, for instance, the view that Jesus's death served as punishment for our sins – that Jesus in effect stood in as our substitute in order to accept the penalty (an idea based on the more ancient Jewish notion that an animal can be sacrificed as a stand-in for a human being). This won't do. If Smith commits a murder and Jones is executed in his place, justice has hardly been served. Nor does it make any difference if Jones volunteers to pay for the crime. Even then, the guilty party remains every bit as deserving of punishment after the execution as before – perhaps more so, in fact, if he now is partially responsible for one more innocent person's death. It follows that our accepting "payment" for our sins – one of the essential features of Christianity – is itself immoral. And the worst thing about all of this is what it implies about God the Father. When it comes to the cross, Christians focus all their attention on Jesus, seemingly never giving a second thought to the other side of the equation. The first member of the trinity is kept conveniently in the background. But was it in fact right for God to *forsake* Jesus? Philosopher Georges Rey uses an interesting method to bring this difficulty to his students' attention. He tells them at the beginning of a class that he has just read about "a local judge who, confronted with a confessed murderer whom he knew and loved," let him go, and killed his own son instead as payment for the crime. "If I tell the story casually enough," Rey continues, "the look of horror and incredulity is striking on the faces of many students who don't immediately see the analogy with the familiar sacrifice of Christ."[86] Rey's made-up story certainly puts a new spin on what is probably the most popular passage in the entire Bible, John 3:16: "For God so loved the world, that he gave his only begotten Son, that whosoever believeth in him should not perish, but have everlasting life." If you read about such a judge in the paper, you would undoubtedly find it shocking. Why then do you regard this biblical verse any differently?

Even if these problems can be resolved, there is the additional difficulty that Jesus's crucifixion does not appear to be sufficient. Now, I don't mean to in any way deny that Jesus suffered, and suffered terribly, on the cross. It was undoubtedly an excruciating experience. But keep in mind that on the traditional view, what the sins of humanity merit is an eternity in hell *for each and every one of us*. The suffering undergone by a single individual over a few hours, no matter how bad, must therefore pale in comparison. Believers also make too much of the fact that Jesus *died* for us. After all, according to them death is merely a journey to another place. Why, then, is it so significant? Even worse, how can this particular death be regarded as a sacrifice at all when Jesus was destined to be resurrected anyway? He may have died for us, but he only remained dead a couple of days. Nor does it solve the problem to say, as Paul does, that the resurrection is proof that the "payment" was accepted by the Father. In fact, that's in stark contradiction to the entire premise: since when does one show that a payment has been accepted *by returning it*?

Finally, and worst of all, there is the matter of the doctrine's real significance. The atonement clearly represents an instance of ritual human sacrifice. Jesus is the "sacrificial lamb" whose death on the cross is thought of as the ultimate offering to God. And though this in no way diminishes the debt we would owe Jesus if he indeed had made himself available for such a purpose, it once again makes the Father look rather bad. Human sacrifice, the ritual taking of innocent lives, is a barbaric concept based on the notion that the gods are bloodthirsty beings who need to be mollified. It is usually associated with primitive religions, and thus something most current believers probably assume the Bible to be against. The story of Abraham and Isaac, revolting as it is, can even be interpreted as repudiating the practice with respect to humans, and replacing it with animal sacrifice. Furthermore, Deuteronomy 18:10 specifically prohibits it. However, the truth of the matter is that Yahweh on other occasions did demand the ritual killing of humans. Numbers 31:28 has God ordering Moses to set aside, "as a tribute to the Lord," one out of every five hundred virgins from the Midianite tribe that God had allowed his warriors to keep as sex slaves. In 40-41, we find out that a total of thirty-two were murdered when "Moses gave the tribute... unto Eleazar the priest, as the Lord commanded Moses." Nor was this sort of thing limited to those captured in war. Exodus 22:29-30 chillingly orders the Israelites to:

> ...not delay to offer the first of thy ripe fruits, and of thy liquors: *the firstborn of thy sons shalt thou give unto me.* Likewise shalt thou do with thine oxen, and with thy sheep... [emphasis added].

The book of Leviticus (in 27:28-29) makes a further reference to this kind of homicide:

> Nothing that a person owns that has been devoted to destruction for the LORD, be it human or animal, or inherited landholding, may be sold or redeemed; every devoted thing is most holy to the LORD. No human beings who have been devoted to destruction can be ransomed; they shall be put to death. [NRSV]

In addition, there is the story of Jephthah, who unintentionally ended up having to sacrifice his only daughter to God (Judges 11:30-39), and of the seven sons of Saul who were killed to appease the Lord (II Samuel 21:1-14). On these occasions, Yahweh for some reason neglected to send an angel to stop the executions, as he did with Isaac.

Apologists emphasize the abandonment of such rituals by God's people, and the final repudiation of all sacrifice brought about by salvation through Jesus. But that doesn't change the fact that the rituals were there to begin with. Moreover, it remains the case that if sacrificing a life for a god is barbaric, then the entire basis for the atonement is as well. It is just another instance of God demanding the murder of a first-born son, since, as Hebrews 9:22 says, there can be no forgiveness of sins "without the shedding of blood". This most central of all Christian concepts is therefore very problematic and, like the concept of hell, provides a moral reason to disavow the religion.

NONBELIEF

God, according to scripture, wants everyone to be saved and to know the truth.[87] In fact, he sacrificed his only son for this very purpose – or so Christianity claims. Nevertheless, the majority of people throughout the last two thousand years have not believed in Jesus, and neither do the majority today. Even worse, Christianity appears to be on the decline. Most human beings seem destined for hell. And yet God is omnipotent; his plan should have been a resounding success. So why hasn't his attempt at salvation been more effective? Nonbelief is one of the greatest difficulties for the Christian. An all-powerful being, it seems, ought to do better. If he really wanted us to believe in him, he could make it happen; he could, for instance, appear in the sky in such a way that all are convinced of his existence. Instead, he is – as Isaiah 45:15 puts it – "a God who hides himself."

Consider the three predominant means he has supposedly used to spread his message: direct revelation, the Bible, and the incarnation. By direct revelation I mean God's making himself heard by, or in some other way known to, specific individuals. The authors of the Bible are one example of those with whom he has reportedly communicated, but there are many others: a great number of people claim that they can directly feel the presence of God, at least on certain occasions. The problem is that this is very weak evidence. How can we be sure that it is really God who is communicating with the believer, especially given that there are other, more plausible, explanations for such things? Note as well that other faiths also report direct revelation from their gods, but that this fact doesn't carry any weight among Christians.

The Bible, supposedly written by individuals who have been inspired by God, suffers from the same weakness: that it is his revelation to mankind is something that must be accepted on faith; there is no evidence whatsoever supporting such a claim. Scripture is of course open to many other criticisms as well, as has been shown throughout this and the previous chapter. But even if it weren't fraught with inconsistencies, falsehoods, and questionable – or downright disturbing – pronounce-ments, it would remain a highly implausible vehicle for the spreading of God's message. And it isn't just that it must be taken on faith. Consider, for instance, that none of the original manuscripts of what eventually came to comprise the Bible have survived. What we have today consists of copies of copies. Often, these contain errors of transcription and of translation. In fact, there are thousands of variations among the surviving manuscripts. Nor are these solely errors due to carelessness. In many instances, changes were made intentionally, as is the case with the ending to Mark mentioned above and with other passages that were added to the original writings. Even the famous story about Jesus stopping the execution of a woman accused of adultery – when he instructed he who is without sin to cast the first stone (John 7:53-8:11) – was not originally in the gospel.[88] There are also many forgeries involved, such as epistles that claim to have been written by Paul but almost certainly were not. In addition, those books that were included in the Bible had to compete with other works that were eventually rejected. This introduces further doubt about the ones that did make it into the official canon. In fact, there is no such thing as *the* Bible; there are several versions around today. Protestants regard some of the books in the Catholic Bible as apocryphal. The Orthodox Church has yet a different compilation of books, as does the Ethiopian Church. No one can be sure that theirs is the right one. Shouldn't God ensure that everyone know, or at least have some means of finding out, which is the true, authorized version of his word?

As to the incarnation, it fares no better. What Jesus did or did not accomplish two thousand years ago provides us with no proof whatsoever that he was God. Consider the resurrection, which is regarded as the most important piece of evidence. The book of Acts reports that, while in Athens, Paul made a speech in which he declared that "God… has given assurance to all by raising [Jesus] from the dead." According to the next passage, "When they heard of the resurrection of the dead, some scoffed."[89] I imagine that many Christians think the Athenians who scoffed at Paul's claim were wrong. But were they? Was it unreasonable of them to doubt what they had been told? Does the resurrection really provide assurance to all? In order to answer this question for yourself, imagine that you are hearing the following story for the first time, even if you have heard it before:

During the first century, in the eastern Mediterranean region, there lived a moral teacher – the son of God, according to some – who reportedly performed many miracles, including healing people, exorcising demons, and once actually bringing a dead person back to life. He had a group of followers, and it is said that he even appeared to some of them after his death. His name was – and this probably isn't what you were expecting – Apollonius of Tyana. (As it turns out, then, it's rather likely that you are in fact hearing this story for the first time.) Apollonius was, however, quite famous for a while, and his wondrous acts were widely celebrated. His life story was written in the third century at the request of the Roman empress Julia Domna, herself a believer. And yet I'm fairly sure you do not accept any of these fantastic stories told about him. True, his admirers claimed these things happened, but that of course is not a sufficient reason to believe them.

But now, suppose that someone told those same Athenians about Apollonius and how he, too, had returned from the grave. Should the Athenians have scoffed at that? If so, then it seems they had every bit as good a reason to doubt Paul. They had no more evidence in the case of Jesus than they had in the case of Apollonius. Of course this by itself does not show that the resurrection of Jesus did not take place. It *could* be (provided we ignore the many problems already discussed) that the gospels report actual events, while Apollonius's biography is full of tall tales. But even if that is the case one must, it seems, admit that the Athenians' skepticism was well-founded. Anyone who insists they should have had faith in what Paul was telling them needs to explain why in that case they should not also have believed a follower of Apollonius – or anyone else reporting similar things, for that matter.

Paul, unfortunately, does not see it that way. He states that God has given his assurance to *all* by raising Jesus from the dead. In other words, he is claiming that the

Athenians, and you and I and everyone else, should know that Jesus is God *because he was resurrected*. That event is supposed to guarantee the truth of the Christian religion. And yet, as we've just seen, it most certainly does not. If the Athenians were reasonable to be skeptical, then Paul was wrong. The evidence provided by God is inadequate, and the claim made in the scriptures that it is adequate is itself false. (It is also a rather ironic claim, given that Paul himself did not become a believer as a result of it, but only after his experience on the road to Damascus. Moreover, Jesus's own followers – and not just Thomas – were doubtful when they first heard reports of the resurrection. And they *knew* Jesus and supposedly saw his miracles! Shouldn't we be at least as skeptical as they?)

Consider, too, that Jesus remained a virtual unknown until well after his death. It was up to his disciples to spread his message. And while there is no doubt that, as religions go, Christianity has been extremely successful, it took almost two millennia for it to reach all corners of the globe, and billions – the majority of humanity – remain unconvinced. Its great success is very much a relative matter. If there were an omnipotent being who wanted us to know about his existence, so that we could decide whether or not to accept his offer of salvation, he would have made things considerably clearer. He would not have resorted to such undependable methods as a collection of writings over which there continue to be disputes and a ministry two thousand years ago that is almost entirely shrouded in mystery.

Given that there is nonbelief, the concept of hell remains problematic no matter how one interprets it – for the question that needs to be answered is why nonbelievers should be regarded as more deserving of punishment (or, what amounts to the same thing, less deserving of forgiveness) than believers. If a person cannot see any evidence for the existence of God, then she cannot believe that Jesus died for her. Why should she be punished merely for failing to know that God is real?

Christians have a handful of (not necessarily mutually exclusive) explanations for the existence of nonbelief. The Oxford philosopher of religion Richard Swinburne, for instance, proposes a solution according to which God needs to remain at a "sufficient distance" to allow us to choose how to behave. Freedom of the will, Swinburne says, is one of the most important gifts God has bestowed on humanity. But if God were to make it absolutely clear that he is watching us, none of us would ever choose to do wrong. And in that case, we wouldn't really be free. Thus, if there is going to be free will, God must remain somewhat hidden.[90]

This of course assumes that the freedom to do the wrong thing is more important than knowing God – a strange claim for a Christian to make. Even if we grant that, however, the problem of unfairness remains. God may have to hide in order to allow us to be completely free, but then why damn all those who fail to believe in him? If it were the case that believers are always virtuous and nonbelievers always wicked, there wouldn't be such a difficulty here. But given that that's not the case, Swinburne's solution is unsatisfactory. It seems that under such circumstances, salvation ought to be based on one's behavior rather than on one's acceptance of Christ.

Another common suggestion, closely related to the above, is that God wants us to be free to choose whether or not to believe, and if he were to appear in the sky to everyone he would be taking away that freedom. He would be *forcing* us to know him. Although God wants us all to believe, he wants us to do so without compulsion.

Therefore, he cannot make his existence completely evident. As philosopher J. P. Moreland put it, "God maintains a delicate balance between keeping his existence sufficiently evident so people will know he's there and yet hiding his presence enough so that people who want to choose to ignore him can do it. This way, their choice of destiny is really free."[91]

In spite of its popularity, this is not a very good argument. For one thing, we do not ordinarily choose what to believe or disbelieve. It is possible that some individuals – maybe even most individuals – are able *in certain cases* to make themselves believe something. For example, a wife may choose to believe that her husband is faithful even when he doesn't appear to be. For the most part, however, beliefs simply happen to us; they form themselves as a result of what we experience. They are no more a matter of choice than are perceptions. And yet we do not feel that our freedom is in any way diminished by this fact. Thus, it makes little sense to maintain that God would be taking away our freedom if he were to reveal his existence. He would not be taking anything away from anyone; he would only be presenting nonbelievers with one more fact about the world – and a very important one at that. Keep in mind, too, that believing God exists and that Jesus is his son is not sufficient; it is accepting his offer of salvation that really matters. Satan and his minions, after all, believe in God. They are in hell not because of disbelief, but because they do not want to submit to their creator. So even if God were to convince everyone that he exists, that would not take away anyone's choice to either accept or reject him. Far from it: it would instead provide those who currently do not believe in him with the chance to make an informed decision. This is a chance that they do not have while they remain nonbelievers. Thus, if God remains hidden, he is needlessly and unfairly condemning many to hell.*

A third explanation is one defended by another already-mentioned religious philosopher, William Lane Craig. He of course agrees that the real issue is not how many people believe in God, but how many accept his offer of salvation. He adds, however, that there "is no reason at all to think that if God were to make his existence more manifest, more people would come into a saving relationship with him."[92] Even if everyone believed in the reality of God, he argues, it wouldn't necessarily follow that a greater number would love God and want to be with him. What God does is make his existence exactly as evident as it needs to be in order to maximize the number of individuals who are saved.

The main thing to note about this suggestion is that it does not at all appear plausible. Those who currently reject Jesus's offer do so, not because they believe in Jesus and decline his gift of eternal bliss, but because they do not believe in Jesus in the first place. How could it possibly be the case, then, that as many or more people would fail to accept God's offer of salvation in a world where all are certain of his existence? God's offer would have to seem pretty unattractive to all of these people, and that's very strange, to say the least. Christians who support this idea usually do so by claiming that nonbelievers would reject God's offer, even if they were convinced he exists, due to

---

* Moreland's argument presupposes that there is such a thing as freedom of the will – something I will present an argument against later. Nevertheless, even without free will as ordinarily understood, there is a difference between deciding something and it happening to us without a decision on our part.

their pride and selfishness. This, however, is a claim that is also central to the fourth and final explanation for the existence of nonbelief, and will therefore be discussed below.

There is another peculiar aspect to Craig's suggestion, though: it makes God into a kind of utilitarian – which coming from a non-utilitarian philosopher is, once again, strange. God, on this view, is merely interested in maximizing the number of saved souls. The reason *why* they are saved is treated as irrelevant. In a situation in which everyone was aware of God's existence, even if fewer were saved, at least they would be the ones who really *merited* salvation – those, in other words, who accepted the offer in full knowledge of what they were getting themselves into. That is the only plan of salvation that takes justice into consideration, the only one that is *fair*. Maximizing the number of the saved irrespective of whether they merit it or not is, by contrast, rather *un*christian.

The proponents of the final suggestion maintain that God is immediately experienced by those whose minds and hearts are open, so that in a sense he *does* reveal his existence to all. The problem, they say, is that not everyone listens. God only succeeds in reaching those who are willing to receive his message. Those who do not wish to hear it – maybe because they would rather continue in their sinful ways – are allowed to ignore it. The influential Christian philosopher Alvin Plantinga defends this view (as does, once again, Craig, for this view is perfectly compatible with the previous one). According to Plantinga, human beings have something called a *sensus divinitatis*, a kind of sixth sense that, when working properly, allows us to be directly aware of God's existence. As a result of sin, however, this sixth sense is currently malfunctioning in many people. Nonbelievers are like the blind and the deaf: they lack an important cognitive capacity.[93] To put it in a slightly different way, God, it is said, determines who will and who will not be aware of his existence based on the kind of life choices we make. Those who choose to live without him – who perhaps would rather be their own masters than submit to his authority – fail to see the signs pointing to his presence. Some add that what God is in fact doing is testing us. He provides just enough evidence to "separate the wheat from the chaff." Nonbelievers are at fault, and hence deserving of punishment, because they are blinded by their own pride and selfishness.

Against such an argument it might appear futile to protest that the evidence for God is poor; the Christian can always reply that the nonbeliever, as a result of her "blindness," is just not a good judge of that evidence. But as it turns out, there are strong objections to this line of reasoning. Throughout this and the previous chapter, numerous reasons were presented in support of the view that the biblical God does not exist. If the Christian apologist wishes to maintain that these reasons are weak, he must explain what is wrong with them. He must show that there are flaws in the logic used or mistakes in the claims made. Merely stating that the nonbeliever is incapable of understanding the truth of Christianity due to her sinful nature is not sufficient. It does not address the fundamental question. The apologist's claim here is no better than that of an atheist who, instead of answering the arguments offered by Christians, simply asserts that the religious believe because they have a need for comforting myths – a need that blinds them to the facts. Maybe that's true, but there is still the work of demonstrating what is wrong with their arguments.

Likewise, even if nonbelievers are blind, the Christian still has to show the mistakes in their reasoning.

A second objection is this. If the apologist is going to maintain that all who reject Christianity do so, not on rational grounds, but because of some character flaw, then it is up to him to present the data that supports this conclusion. As it turns out, however, there is no reason to suppose that those who are irreligious commit more crimes, are more dishonest, or are less kind than the average. Many studies have been conducted, and in some respects the religious have come off better than the non-religious while in other respects the opposite is the case. In none has there been any great difference.

Finally, the notion that failure to accept God's message is a result of sinfulness ignores one very obvious fact: those who do not believe in Jesus are not limited to atheists and agnostics. The majority who reject Christianity are followers of competing religions – and most of them (just like Christians) have the beliefs they do for no other reason than because of where they were born. But surely the proponent of the above argument is not claiming that sin is in some way correlated with geographical location?

When we consider all of the problems we have covered in this chapter – the lack of evidence, the mythical elements and contradictions, the existence of nonbelief, the unjustifiability of salvation through Christ, the difficulties associated with the concepts of the atonement and of hell – and add to this already long list the problems discussed in the previous chapter, one thing seems clear: the only possible reason left for believing in the Christian God is an emotional one. It certainly cannot be defended rationally. To any impartial observer, the divinity of Jesus is on a par with the existence of Zeus, Thor, or Quetzalcoatl.

4

EVIL AND

THE PERFECT BEING

> Is he willing to prevent evil, but not able? Then is
> he impotent. Is he able, but not willing? Then is he
> malevolent. Is he both able and willing? Whence
> then is evil?
>
> – Hume, *Dialogues Concerning Natural Religion*

According to most theists, God is the greatest possible
being: all-powerful, all-knowing, perfectly good, eternal,
omnipresent, and several other things besides. Defining
God as perfect in every respect ensures that nothing can
be greater. It also means that God can always be counted
upon, that we can put our trust completely in him. Some
will go so far as to maintain that only such a being is truly
worthy of worship – or even that nothing less can be called

God. The concept of a perfect being brings with it certain difficulties, however. In this chapter, we will look at the central problem associated with belief in such an entity, the problem of evil. Its basic idea may be stated as follows:

> God is all-knowing, all-powerful, and all-good. Now, since God is all-knowing, he is aware of any evil that occurs; since he is all-powerful, he can put a stop to any evil; and since he is all-good, he wants there to be no evil. If there were a God, therefore, he would stop all evil. And yet, there is evil — and plenty of it. Therefore, God does not exist.

This is an old problem, going at least as far back as the ancient Greek philosopher Epicurus, but in spite of that it is still widely discussed. Charles Templeton, a former preacher and close associate of Billy Graham, famously lost his faith because of it. Writers from C. S. Lewis to Harold Kushner to Bart Ehrman have published books about it, and in a recent work new atheist critic Dinesh D'Souza even appealed to the latest science in search of an answer.[94] It's not likely to go away anytime soon. In fact, it is probably the most common reason offered in defense of atheism; William Lane Craig even calls it "atheism's killer argument."[95] And it is something that is taken very seriously because, to anyone who has thought about it, it's obvious that there is a real difficulty here. A world in which millions die of hunger, in which wars kill millions more, and in which even small children are stricken with terminal cancer does not appear to have been created by a loving and supremely powerful being.

Before considering proposed solutions to this problem, however, we need to clarify what it means to say that God is all-powerful, for this supposed characteristic of the supreme being is often thought of in a way that is too strong and ends up being nonsensical. Often, omnipotence is taken to imply no limitations of any kind — not even logical ones. Even worse, some theists who are certain that there are no limits whatsoever to what God can do also inconsistently claim that he couldn't have created a world just like ours without allowing evil in it. In the next section we will see a way to interpret the concept of omnipotence that avoids these errors.

SQUARE CIRCLES AND MARRIED BACHELORS

If God is omnipotent, then in some sense he can do anything. But what does it mean to say that God can do anything? Could he create a married bachelor, say, or a square circle? Married bachelors and square circles are logical impossibilities — contradictions in terms. Consider the former. A bachelor is an unmarried man. A married bachelor, then, would be a married unmarried man, and these characteristics obviously cancel each other out. One can be married or unmarried, but certainly not both. Thus, the very meaning of the word "bachelor" rules out the idea of a married one. Similarly for "square circle," since the definitions of "square" and "circle" describe mutually incompatible geometrical shapes. And there are many other examples of logical impossibility. It is impossible for two plus two to equal five, for a sister to have no siblings, or for something red to be colorless. Such logical impossibilities are different from things that are merely *physically* impossible, in other words, from things that are ruled out by the laws of nature. It is impossible for a human being to walk on water as Jesus is said to have done, but no logical impossibility is involved here. If the laws of nature were altered, water might support the weight of a man — and a virgin might give birth, and someone might be brought back from the dead. One is able to make sense out of such claims provided one assumes that different laws apply in their case (or what amounts to the same thing, that the usual laws are suspended). But one cannot make sense out of a triangle with four sides or out of a god-believing atheist, since what these describe is internally contradictory. So, to return to our question, can God create a married bachelor? And if not, does that mean that he is not really omnipotent?

Many theists think that in fact God can do literally *anything*, including the logically impossible. They perhaps fear that if one denies God's ability to create square circles and such things, then one is somehow diminishing God. That is a mistake. It is perfectly consistent to claim, on the one hand, that someone is omnipotent and, on the other, that he cannot do anything involving a contradiction. God's inability to create logical impossibilities does not in any way detract from his power. The reason even an all-powerful being cannot create a married bachelor is that the term "married bachelor" fails to describe a possible entity — and similarly for other internally inconsistent terms. Thus, the claim that God cannot create a married bachelor is not the claim that there might be *something*, namely one of these strange married yet single individuals, that God could create *if only he were more powerful*. Instead, it is the claim that the logically impossible simply cannot be, period. The problem is not with any lack in God's power, but rather with the term "married bachelor."

To say that God is omnipotent, therefore, is to say, at most, that he can do *anything that is logically possible*.

For those who remain unconvinced, an analogy might help. Consider the parallel claim that God is all-knowing. This implies that, in some sense, God knows everything. But does it mean he *knows*, for example, that Billy Graham was a devil worshipper? Obviously not. We reject such a suggestion because we realize that knowledge is something one can have only of truths. One cannot know falsehoods. (Of course, people often *claim* to know things that aren't true: e.g., some people "know" that 9/11 was an inside job. But in such cases, they do not have real knowledge; they have only the illusion of knowledge.) So God does not know things that are false, but that is not a problem: he still knows everything that is *knowable*, and that is enough to make him omniscient. Similarly, God cannot do the logically impossible, but again there's no problem: he still can do everything that is *doable* – and that is enough for omnipotence. Logical impossibilities aren't any more doable than falsehoods are knowable.

THE TRADITIONAL PROBLEM OF EVIL

With the above clarification in place, we are ready to examine the principal obstacle to belief in a perfect God. It must be said that, even though the difficulty is a serious one, many theists tend to dismiss it without giving it much thought, almost as if the solution is obvious. But even though there have been many different attempts to get around the problem, none are truly convincing, as we'll see.

A few theists deny that God is perfect. Perhaps he is not all-powerful, as Rabbi Harold Kushner claims in his bestselling book, *When Bad Things Happen to Good*

People; or perhaps he is not concerned with the fate of human beings, and is therefore indifferent to our suffering. Of course if either of these is the case, then we are no longer dealing with the deity who is the subject of this chapter. Thus, although a God who is not perfect is certainly a possibility, it is a possibility we will put aside for now.* It should be pointed out, however, that merely denying God's omnipotence, omniscience, or absolute goodness is far from satisfactory as a reply to the problem of evil. Take the view that he is not omnipotent, and so cannot prevent all evil. Even if that is the case, he is still inconceivably powerful. Perhaps he cannot put a stop to *every* instance of evil, but a being capable of creating an entire universe ought to be able to do something about, say, a mass murderer whose killing spree lasts for several years. Surely the creator of the universe cannot be so helpless as to be unable to give a particular human being a fatal case of pneumonia or some such affliction. Merely denying God's omnipotence, then, is not enough – and this is tantamount to claiming that the problem of evil also applies, to some extent, to the question of the existence of less-than-perfect deities.

The view that God is indifferent to the well-being of his creatures is also difficult to accept, unless accompanied by the idea that he is so detached from his creation as to not even be aware of us. Otherwise, his lack of concern would more accurately be described as extreme callousness. Nero is criticized for allegedly fiddling while Rome burned; a God who ignored the plight of the millions upon millions who have died as a result of disease, natural disasters, and

---

* Such lesser deities will be covered by later chapters (which address theism in a more general sense).

wars, even though he could easily have prevented the whole thing, would be far worse.

One may also deny the other main premise of the argument, the claim that there is evil. This, however, is if anything an even less satisfactory solution. It is true that many Hindus, for instance, maintain that the suffering we see around us is illusory. Presumably, it is part of the "world of appearance," and not part of reality. But such skepticism is utterly unrealistic. Moreover, even if we suppose that our perceptions are mistaken, it remains the case that we do experience them. And our experiences cannot logically be doubted to exist *at least within us*. Think about the experience you are having at this very moment. If you are a real skeptic, you might seriously entertain the thought that you are not currently reading a book, but are instead sound asleep and having a very vivid dream. Maybe this book does not even exist; maybe it is only a figment of your rather active imagination. But even if that were true, it is undeniable that you are having the experience you are having. Whether dream or reality, you are experiencing *this*. Likewise, whether illusory or not, the *experience* of evil exists. But that experience is itself a bad thing: you would be better off without it. It is not good that you are made unhappy by seeing what appear to be starving people in Africa (even if admittedly that isn't nearly as bad as there actually being starving people). So the existence of evil cannot be denied this way. Similarly, the common objection that evil is not a "positive reality," but only the *absence* of goodness (much as darkness is only the absence of light) is entirely unhelpful. Such a move merely redefines the terms without substantively changing anything. A perfect God would no more allow such an absence of goodness than he would "actual" evil.

Most theists of course accept the premises of the argument; they suppose both that God is all-powerful, all-knowing, and all-good, *and* that there is such a thing as evil. Their only alternative, then, is to dispute the reasoning in the argument. They must, in other words, claim that evil does not rule out a perfect God – that suffering and injustice are in fact compatible with his existence. On such a view, those who insist that God would not allow anything bad in the universe are simply mistaken. And if that is the case, then the atheistic conclusion does not follow, and need not be accepted.

Though it may not appear so at first, the theist who argues in this way is – strictly speaking – correct. The existence of God is not inconsistent with the existence of evil, *provided there is a morally sufficient reason for God allowing that evil*. Some of it may be allowed, for instance, if it is necessary in order to prevent an equal or even greater evil, or if it is the only way to bring about some great good – one that more than compensates for the evil in question. God's existence, then, is not incompatible with evil itself; it is only incompatible with *gratuitous* evil – in other words, with bad things that serve no greater moral purpose. The traditional argument therefore does not conclusively rule God out.

It seems extremely unlikely, nonetheless, that *every* evil we see around us is justified in the above way. There's just too much suffering and too much misery for all of it to be necessary. Just consider some of the statistics on this. According to U. N. estimates, as many as seventeen thousand children die of hunger *every single day*.[96] Each year, millions more die of easily preventable diseases, sometimes because they simply lack clean drinking water. Malaria, HIV, tuberculosis, and many other maladies continue to have devastating effects in many places around the world. The prevalence of evil therefore provides us with at least very strong evidence that God does not exist. It may not disprove the existence of God, but it definitely makes his existence highly improbable – so improbable, in fact, that we can say with assurance that there is no God.

Most atheist philosophers nowadays are content to leave it at that. They see the argument from evil as providing us with a very strong reason to deny the existence of a perfect being, even if it falls short of conclusive proof. Below, however, I will argue that there are in fact at least some evils that are strictly incompatible with the existence of a perfect God – and which therefore provide us with definitive evidence that he isn't there. I will argue, in other words, that there clearly are some unjustified evils in this world. Thus, even though evil *per se* is compatible with a perfect God, some of the evils around us are not.

FREE WILL

Most theists, of course, disagree that the vast quantity of evil around us makes the existence of God unlikely – much less that it proves he does not exist. They maintain that, at least in principle, all of that evil can be explained one way or another. And by far the most common theistic reply along such lines is the appeal to free will, the view that, because God gave human beings freedom of choice, we have the option of doing the wrong thing – and that unfortunately many of us do just that.* As C. S. Lewis put

---

* The kind of free will that is meant here, and throughout this book, is what philosophers call "libertarian freedom," which implies that under normal circumstances more than

it, "Some people think they can imagine a creature which was free but had no possibility of going wrong; I cannot. If a thing is free to be good it is also free to be bad."[97] Osama bin Laden and his accomplices could have put their God-given abilities to different use, but they were free to pursue the ends they desired, and the result was the death of thousands. Free will, then, is what allowed evil to be introduced into creation.

One might suppose that in that case things would have been better had God decided against giving us such freedom. Not according to this argument, however: if we did not have free will, we would essentially be pre-programmed automatons, and life would lose all of its meaning. God wanted to create persons in his own image, individuals capable of making moral choices and able to freely accept or reject him. The price we have to pay for this power, unfortunately, is the evil that can result. Still, according to this view, it is entirely worth it. Free will is such a valuable commodity that it more than makes up for all of its regrettable consequences.

Now, one thing that it is important to realize about such an argument is that it asks us to suppose that God had, in effect, a choice to make. God could have created a world without free creatures *and* without evil in it, but chose instead to make one with free will and at least the possibility of evil. The argument therefore assumes that there are certain things even God cannot do. It is based on the idea that God cannot create a world with free creatures *and at the same time guarantee that none will ever sin.* And yet, as previously mentioned, this argument is made by many theists who also maintain that nothing is impossible for God – theists who say that he could make

---

one course of action is possible to each of us.

married bachelors and single wives. But if God could do *that*, then there is no reason why he couldn't also create free-willed creatures who are guaranteed to never go wrong. It doesn't matter if one cannot understand how God might accomplish such a feat: if he can do anything – if he can do even the logically impossible – then he certainly can do this. And if that's the case, the existence of evil remains a problem. To consistently apply the free will argument, then, the theist must admit that there are logical impossibilities, actions that even an omnipotent being cannot perform. (In addition, the theist must maintain that it is in fact logically impossible for there to be free-willed beings that are guaranteed to never sin. But as we'll see shortly, that too – in spite of what Lewis said – raises a difficulty.)

All of this of course assumes that the appeal to free will is a reasonable answer to the argument from evil, which is something that has yet to be established. In fact, although it is very popular, it is a very weak attempt to solve the problem. It is undeniable that for many it is an attractive solution, of course. Nearly everyone believes in freedom of the will, and putting the blame on us – or even better, on others – may seem to be the perfect way to get God off the hook. Human beings are far from perfect, after all, and it is an incontrovertible fact that a great number of terrible things occur as a result of our species' moral deficiencies. From that realization to the conclusion that perhaps all of the world's problems are our fault is but a short step. But unfortunately, it's not quite that simple.

The first issue that needs to be addressed is just how much can be blamed on the actions of free-willed creatures. When most theists consider the problem of evil, they tend to limit their attention to the existence of *moral* evil. This may largely be due to the name of the problem.

"Evil" is a word that in ordinary discourse is reserved for moral agents and their activities. Events and situations that no one is responsible for do not qualify. Thus, bin Laden was evil, but hurricane Andrew was not. Earthquakes, tornados, droughts, cancers, and many other such things are natural occurrences, not things brought about by any moral agent. And if the object is to account for the existence of *moral* evil, the free will defense may appear fully adequate. But of course the problem is not limited to moral evil. A perfect God is inconsistent with the existence of any gratuitous suffering, with any unjustified bad thing whatsoever. Thus, if free will is the explanation, then it must be the case that, in addition to wars and crime, freedom of choice brings about disease and natural disasters. But how can that be? How can a hurricane be something that occurs because God gave some of his creatures free will?

One possibility is to blame God's old nemesis, the devil. When more than two hundred thousand people were killed on a single day in the 2004 Asian tsunami, minister Franklin Graham, struggling to make sense out of such a tragedy, reminded Christians that the god of this world is Satan. The theory here, which finds biblical support,[98] states that for the time being the devil is in charge, although eventually God will return and set things right again. Of course, in order for this theory to be accepted, one must believe in the existence not just of God, but of at least one additional supernatural being – and the more assumptions that go into a theory, the weaker it becomes. Is there any reason to believe that Satan is real? I used to imagine that hardly anyone nowadays could believe in such an absurd concept, but as it turns out, 60% of Americans claim to believe in the devil – though it should be said that as many as half of these believers may not really think of him as a personal being, but instead as an "impersonal force that influences people to do wrong."[99] At any rate, and irrespective of what opinions the general public may hold, the theist who takes this route is asking others to buy into even more facts for which he ought to provide the evidence. Even worse, the introduction of God's rival doesn't really help, since the central difficulty has yet to be accounted for. Why would God allow the devil to act freely? He could easily intervene and prevent his former associate from causing such havoc. What justifies God's passivity? This, however, is a difficulty that plagues the free will argument with respect to the actions of human beings as well, and thus one to which we will return below.

One may also maintain that the sinfulness of humans is the underlying reason for the natural evils in the world. Whether the story of the Fall is taken literally or figuratively, the idea is that, since we are disobedient to our creator, he has placed us in an environment that is fraught with pain and suffering. As God declares in Genesis 3:17, "Because thou... hast eaten of the tree, of which I commanded thee, saying, 'Thou shalt not eat of it': cursed is the ground..." This view can be combined with the previous one: the devil is granted free rein because we are sinners, and deserving of being punished. Theists tend to hold that the wicked are particularly prone to this sort of divine retribution, of course. Evangelist Pat Robertson informed us that hurricane Katrina was sent to our shores as a result of God's disapproval of legalized abortion, and made similarly callous remarks about a more recent earthquake in Haiti.* Nor is he by any means alone, of

---

* Robertson and his friend Jerry Falwell also said this sort of thing regarding the September 11 terrorist attacks.

course: claims of this kind have been around for centuries. But if sinfulness is the basis for such events, how does one explain the haphazard nature of the punishment? As the biblically-based saying goes, it rains on the just and the unjust alike.[100] Job was a very pious man, but that did not stop God from destroying everything he had and even killing his children. (In fact, it was ultimately *because* he was so pious that these terrible things were done to him!) In addition, I'm sure that among the many victims of hurricane Katrina were quite a few pro-lifers, and probably even some fans of Pat Robertson.

A view that is more consistent with the facts is that bad things happen because we are *all* to a certain degree sinners, and thus all deserving of God's wrath. At least in that case the injustice is not quite as incomprehensible. It is still problematic, though: if we are all deserving of punishment, why is it administered so unevenly? Why do some have wonderful lives while others have a miserable time? Even more difficult to explain is the suffering and death of infants. The doctrine of original sin, which is the traditional explanation in their case, has unfortunately never made it clear just how newborns can be guilty of disobedience to God. And it is not just infants that pose a problem. Original sin also fails to account for the existence of animal suffering. Animals are not moral agents, hence cannot be guilty of anything. Why, then, should they also experience pain? Are we to suppose that God is simply callous toward them? Moreover, when a natural disaster occurs, we think of it as a tragedy; but if all the victims had it coming – if they *deserved* their punishment – then we should not think of it as a bad thing at all. At most, we should feel a sense of relief that it happened to them instead of us. This shows the inconsistency that is all too often inherent in theistic attempts to justify such events.

The existence of natural evils, then, is a problem for which the appeal to free will offers no adequate solution. But a second flaw with the free will argument is that it cannot even account for the existence of all *moral* evil. Most theists hold that God has perfect knowledge of the future in spite of human free will. In other words, they maintain that, although we are free, God knows what we are going to do before we even decide to do it. But if so, then God could obviously prevent all evil acts. And even if he cannot predict every decision we are going to make, nevertheless, as an omniscient being, he is at least able to see human intentions as soon as they are formed. That is, once a decision to act exists in someone's mind, God knows about it. Moreover, God can intervene immediately, before the intention is carried out. He may not be able to prevent Joe the murderer from suddenly desiring to pull the trigger of a gun, but he can prevent the actual killing: he can cause the gun to jam, or an anvil to drop on Joe's head, or any of a number of things that would spare the victim. So once again – and this applies whether the perpetrator of an evil deed is human or Satan – what justifies God's passivity? In order to account for all of the murders, rapes, kidnappings, and every other crime that has ever occurred, the theist must maintain that there is some justification for God allowing them – a justification that goes beyond the mere existence of free will.

An informed believer might at this point suppose that I'm misinterpreting the argument from free will. The standard theistic response to the above is to maintain that freedom would not really count for much if God interfered in our lives so as to keep us from doing wrong. That is, bad people might still form bad intentions, but if they were not allowed to carry them out, then they wouldn't *really* be free – not in any meaningful sense. (And again, similarly for Satan; this would explain why he is allowed to send epidemics and earthquakes our way whenever he feels like it.) It is not the mere fact of free will, then, but the ability to put it into practice that matters. But is that really true? Must freedom entail the ability to do terrible things? A little reflection shows that it does not. Suppose that God did not allow bad actions. We would still be free to choose to do this or that, provided neither alternative was harmful to others. People form governments and put in place law enforcement agencies in order to prevent evildoers from committing wrongful acts, and hardly anyone thinks that this constitutes an unjustified violation of criminals' freedom to act. Why, then, should God's interference be regarded any differently? If it is right for human beings to stop crime in its tracks, why isn't it right for God to do so as well? Or, to make the same point in a more graphic way, if you saw a sadistic criminal about to brutally rape and murder a small child and yet did nothing – even though you could have stopped him without so much as incurring danger to yourself – your behavior would be utterly inexcusable. Why, then, do some theists argue that God's inaction in such cases is *perfectly justified*? Surely the freedom of the evil rapist in this case is not so important as to outweigh the safety and welfare of the child. I might also add that the biblical God, for one, does not always refrain from intruding in our affairs. The destruction of Sodom and Gomorrah is but one example of divine justice found in the Bible. If the freedom to act in whatever way we please is so important, why then did God put a stop to what the individuals in those two cities were doing? Or send a hurricane to punish those who believe in a woman's right to choose?

So far we have seen that the free will solution contains unresolved problems with respect to natural evil and even with respect to moral evil. A third flaw with it is its incompatibility with other beliefs held by most theists. Above, I pointed out that in order for the argument to go through in the first place, one must suppose that God had a choice to make: either create a sinless world, or create free creatures. One cannot have both. This means that, as Lewis indicated, it must be logically impossible for there to be free-willed creatures who are guaranteed to never sin. And yet, the theist's own view goes against this, for it supposes that there are morally perfect free beings. God himself is supposed to be such a being, as is the human Jesus. In addition, if heaven is a place that is free from sin, it seems all of us must be capable of existing in such an unblemished state. Either free persons there never commit wrongs or else there are no free persons there. And the latter makes no sense if freedom is essential to a meaningful existence, as the free will argument requires. Freedom, then, must be compatible with moral perfection. It follows that God should have been able to create a world filled with sinless, free creatures.

A second point to note is this. As I've already mentioned, most theists hold that God has perfect knowledge of the future in spite of human free will. But now, if God knows the future, then he knows all of the evil acts that are going to be perpetrated by his free-willed creatures. It follows that he could have created only free-willed creatures that he knew would *not* in fact choose to perform evil acts. They may have been capable of doing wrong, may even have been tempted to do so, but would all have resisted the temptation. And if that is the case, then why was Charles Manson born? Even worse, if all of us are sinners, why did he make *any* of us? The upshot of all this is that, if the free will solution is the answer to the problem of evil, then to be consistent the believer must admit that God does not have complete knowledge of the future. The theist cannot have it both ways. She cannot consistently maintain both that God knows what free-willed creatures are going to do and that he could not have avoided the evil acts performed by some of these creatures. There is a glaring contradiction lying at the very heart of orthodox Christianity here. The idea that even God does not know the future completely is therefore one that believers perhaps should not dismiss out of hand.

All of the above is more than enough to show that the appeal to free will is inadequate. There is a fourth main objection, though: that there is no such thing as free will at all. Obviously, if the freedom in question does not even exist, then neither can it be the explanation for the existence of evil. A defense of this claim, however, will be postponed until the last chapter, as it is a central part of the final argument in this book.

NECESSARY EVILS AND INEVITABLE CONSEQUENCES

If free will is not the answer, might there be some other solution? Many have been proposed. For instance, there is the idea that evil is necessary for our moral development. It provides us with the opportunity to become compassionate, courageous, just, and so on. Without others who need our help, and without challenges in our own lives, we would not acquire virtues such as these. As some who defend this view have argued, God wants us to develop into the kind of persons who are worthy of spending eternity with him, and the only way to accomplish that is to place us in a world containing a certain amount of misery and suffering. Only then will we mature morally to the point where we will be deserving of our heavenly reward. The mistake made by the proponent of the argument from evil is to assume that God's purpose in creating us was solely to make us happy. If that had been his intention, he would of course have created a perfect paradise for us to live in. But that is not what God had in mind. Rather, his plan was to create a place where we could grow and develop to the point where we could freely accept or reject him. Or so some theists argue.

Unfortunately, any attempt to apply this line of reasoning to specific cases demonstrates how implausible it really is. Here's one example. According to the influential religious philosopher Richard Swinburne, every single death that occurred in Hiroshima's atomic blast served a moral purpose. As Swinburne himself put it, if "one less person had been burnt by the Hiroshima atomic bomb... there would have been less opportunity for courage and sympathy..."[101] (And just think how awful *that* would have been!) And as if that weren't bad enough, in *The God Delusion*, Dawkins reports that during a television panel discussion with him, Swinburne defended the Holocaust in a similar way, as "offering the Jews a wonderful opportunity to be courageous and noble."[102] Now, these are – to put it mildly – rather incredible statements. But this is the sort of thing that one must say in order to use this kind of excuse for evil: there must be some reason, after all, for God allowing such terrible events. Swinburne should at least be praised for being consistent.

Of course there are good reasons, besides simple astonishment, to disagree with such disturbing thinking. In the first place, it seems God could accomplish the same result – and even better results – without nearly so much suffering. Is it really necessary, for instance, to have millions of starving children in the world – who, incidentally, are hardly ever in the minds of those comfortably living thousands of miles away? A few strategically placed poor children in our own midst would be far more effective as a way of rousing our compassion (plus they could receive immediate help). Furthermore, great misfortune often makes people more cynical rather than more courageous, and is more apt to produce despair than to inspire charity. In many cases, it even turns people away from God. Thus, if the point is to encourage our development, it must be said that this simply isn't a very good plan. By Swinburne's logic, God is at best a bumbling and dangerous incompetent.

The proponent of this view must also maintain that a world with both compassion and suffering is preferable to a world with neither; and likewise for one with both courage and danger, temperance and excess, and so on. But why should that be? Such things as compassion and courage are virtues only *because* there is suffering and danger. In their absence, they would hardly be missed. We are so used to thinking of compassion, for instance, as an indispensable virtue that it is difficult to imagine it being unnecessary. However, in a universal paradise, where every conscious being experiences only good things, why would anyone have reason to pity others? Wouldn't it be enough that they love one another? All of this suggests that it would be better to have neither suffering nor compassion than to have both – and similarly for other such combinations as danger and courage.

So much for this view. An even less plausible reply to the problem of evil is to maintain that every bad thing that happens is an inevitable consequence of the good things that God created. Consider pain. It exists for a reason: it serves the function of warning an organism that something is wrong, and of causing the organism to take immediate action if possible. Thus, according to the proponent of this view, God was justified in creating both human and animal suffering. Or, to take a different example, hurricanes and tornados bring about terrible devastation, but they are, it is claimed, an unavoidable consequence of a world in which a complex climatic system operates so as to produce the conditions necessary for our existence. One very amusing excuse along such lines was made by a caller to the cable access show *The Atheist Experience*, who argued that God created earthquakes so that minerals can be mixed around in the earth's crust![103] And claims of a similar nature were more recently made by Dinesh D'Souza in his book *What's So Great about God.*[104]

It must be said that those who argue in these ways suffer from a rather extreme failure of the imagination. It is true that pain serves a biological function. But that is because organisms are the product of evolution, a process that cares nothing about their suffering. To suppose that an omnipotent being could not find any other means of achieving the same ends, however, is ridiculous. For one thing, he could have made animals in such a way that they just automatically know when they need to take evasive action. And there are even better proposals than that. God could have taken care of all of his creatures' needs in an environment free of predators, disease, wildfires, or hurricanes; he could have created a world with no danger in it whatsoever, one without even the possibility of injury. The entire universe could consist of heaven, and nothing else. Beings in such a world would have no need for a warning system to protect them. And there certainly wouldn't be any need for minerals to be mixed around in that environment. This "inevitable consequences" argument therefore fails as well.

The existence of heaven is itself often appealed to as an answer to the problem of evil, the idea being that any calamities experienced in this life will be more than made up for by the eternal happiness in the hereafter. However, as already suggested above, God could have placed us directly into heaven, and that of course would be preferable to our suffering first and only afterwards getting into paradise. Consider an infant who dies from a painful disease. The fact that this child ends up in heaven, if it is a fact, does not justify the agony she experiences beforehand. God could have made her death painless, at the very least – although even that would leave us with a problem regarding the suffering of the child's parents, among others. So once again, this is not an adequate response.

A view which does have some initial plausibility, even though it too is flawed, is that goodness could not exist without evil – or at least that we could not be *aware* of good without having the experience of evil. Imagine what it would be like if everything were green. We would not really notice it. In order for us to be cognizant of the fact that something is green, there must be another color to provide some contrast. By analogy, it is alleged that if everything were perfect, no one would realize it, and there could be no true happiness. There has to be something to counterbalance the good.

This idea gets some support from the fact that people aren't usually made happy simply by getting everything too easily. Having to strive for a goal, having to put some effort into what we do, appears to be more conducive to human well-being. Whether it *had* to be that way is harder to say. At any rate, none of this justifies evil. Green does not have to be contrasted with red, its opposite, in order to be noticed; blue will do just fine. Likewise, good does not require evil as a counterpart; it is sufficient to have things that are merely neutral, neither good nor bad. It is even possible to distinguish among different levels of goodness, just as it is possible to detect different shades of green. Perhaps God could have created a universe in which our lives are sometimes extremely happy, and at other times merely somewhat pleasant. The high points would still be appreciated. To suggest, on the other hand, that millions of people must die horrible, painful deaths in order for the good things in life to be enjoyed is patently absurd.

Finally, some theists, as a last resort, admit that none of the solutions provided so far is satisfactory. However, they say, this doesn't mean there isn't *some* explanation. We may simply not know what the real reason for the existence of evil is. Why should we suppose that we'd be able to understand God's intentions? We are mere human beings, tiny creatures on a rather small, insignificant planet, living but for a moment in an immense, possibly eternal universe. For all we know, everything that happens here today is necessary for some great good in the far off future. We must keep in mind that even the tiniest of events may turn out to have enormous repercussions. In chaos theory this is known as the "butterfly effect," named after the idea that a single butterfly beating its wings could be one of the causes of a hurricane. (For instance, the sudden movement of its wings may startle a wildebeest, who begins to run, causing the rest of the herd to do the same, in turn creating a dust cloud over the plains of Africa that may be a factor in the formation of a tropical storm which eventually brings devastation to the Caribbean. Without that one apparently insignificant event, none of the rest would have followed.) Maybe, then, every single incident that we consider bad is something that God must allow so as to produce some great benefit, or to prevent some great disaster, later on.

What the theist who makes the above claim fails to take into account, however, is that God controls the very laws of nature. Some undesirable events may be necessary if certain consequences are to occur naturally *given the causal laws and the initial conditions in the actual universe.* But what if these laws or conditions had been different? It is unclear why God couldn't have made a universe with laws designed to bring about desirable outcomes by fully tolerable means. Furthermore, according to the theist, God can ensure just about any future state of affairs directly, even in the universe as it is, simply by performing a miracle. There is no need of a complex causal chain, especially one involving misery and pain. Thus, in order for an evil to be justified by some later occurrence there must be a *logical* – and not merely a causal – connection between the two events. In other words, it must be the case that without the evil, the later occurrence would be absolutely ruled out. Only then can we say that even an omnipotent being would have no alternative but to allow that evil. Now, in cases involving human suffering, the theist can often tell a somewhat plausible story as to why the suffering is necessary. One cannot learn to overcome adversity in a perfect paradise, for example. But this strategy does not work so well in cases involving animal suffering. And that brings us to a new way of demonstrating that a perfect God does not exist. As I mentioned above, there are some evils that can be shown to be unjustified – evils that God cannot possibly have a reason for allowing, and that therefore are strictly incompatible with the existence of a perfect being. In the next section, this claim is defended. And what this will show is that a perfect God is not just highly unlikely, but is in fact impossible.

A NEW ARGUMENT FROM EVIL

There are millions of starving people in the world, millions more dying of easily preventable diseases, and millions who have died in horrible, painful circumstances throughout history. To focus on the suffering of a single animal as part of an argument against the existence of God might therefore seem unreasonable. Even animal lovers must admit that, next to all that human misery, an individual animal's fate doesn't count for much. But to think this way is to miss the point of the argument I'm about to present. Its logic has nothing to do with the amount of suffering involved. Rather, it has to do with the lack of justification for that suffering. The point to keep in mind is that a perfect God by definition cannot allow even the smallest amount of evil unless it is in some way justified – unless, that is, it is necessary for some greater good or to prevent some equally bad or worse evil. And yet it is relatively easy to show that some evils in this world cannot be justified in this way.

Consider – to borrow an example from philosopher William Rowe – a fawn that is seriously burned in a natural forest fire, suffers terrible pain for several days, and then dies. Who benefits from this event? Could it be the fawn? It seems clear that cannot be the case: unlike a human being, the fawn cannot learn some valuable lesson, such as something about courage or compassion, as a result of its situation. And what else is there that could possibly be regarded as a benefit for this creature? In order to benefit from it, it would have to be in some way changed for the better by it, and that is simply not the case. (Although it is implausible, some might argue that even excruciating pain could serve an animal some purpose, such as keeping it from behaving in a way that would cause further injury or prevent recovery. But even if we grant this it doesn't apply to the current case, since we have stipulated that the fawn dies as a result of its injuries.) If anyone gains anything from the event, then, it must be someone other than the animal. One possibility, as we've already seen, is that, unbeknownst to anyone other than God, the suffering of the fawn sets up a causal chain that eventually brings about a highly desirable result. Another possibility is that a person learns something valuable from the event. Perhaps someone who finds out about the poor creature becomes more humane as a result, and this leads to consequences that more than make up for the fawn's agony.

But here's the catch: since God can control what happens to the animal internally, he could make it the case that the fawn merely *appears* to suffer, while keeping everything else the same. The fawn's behavior could be consistent with a real case of suffering, while in reality the animal feels no pain at all. Such a thing is undeniably possible given that pain — like all mental experiences — is an internal, private matter. And since the behavior would be the same, the causal chain started by the animal's movements would be unaffected, although in this case it would have its origin, not in the animal's actual suffering, but in a small manipulation performed by God on its nervous system. Similarly, any observable effects which might teach someone a lesson in compassion would remain unaffected. All of this is possible for an omnipotent being. But in that case, the animal's pain cannot be justified. It is pointless. Any benefit that results from it could have come about without it. This cannot be denied given that pain is an internal experience that only the sufferer can be directly aware of. It follows that if animals really do suffer in this way, then God does not exist. But we all know that animals do in fact suffer in this way. We have almost as good a reason for believing this about animals as we have for believing that fellow human beings experience pain. The behavior of animals attests to the fact, and their physiology, at least in the case of other vertebrates, is sufficiently similar to ours to make it ridiculous to suppose otherwise.

The argument, then, is this. If animals experience terrible, prolonged pain, and if they do not learn a valuable lesson (e.g., about courage or compassion) from their experience, then their pain cannot be justified, for anything else that is a desirable consequence of that pain could be achieved without the pain in the first place. But it is obvious that animals do experience such pain and do not learn valuable lessons or benefit in any other way from it – especially in cases where they end up dying as a result of their wounds. Therefore, there are unjustified evils in the world.

Now, when we began discussing the problem of evil, we saw that there are those who avoid the entire problem by denying the existence of evil itself, and a similar move might be attempted by the theist here. He might claim that *in fact* God performs a miracle each time an animal is injured, so that the animal only appears to be in distress. However, it is almost as absurd to deny that there is animal suffering such as that in the current scenario as it is to deny that there is evil. Such a denial goes against all of the evidence that we have and has no other basis than the theist's desire to avoid the problem posed by its existence. The only reasonable conclusion one can draw is that at least much of the evil in our world cannot be justified. There is a lot of gratuitous misery and suffering out there, and that is simply the way things are. But in that case, there cannot be an all-powerful, all-knowing, all-good being. There cannot be a perfect God who cares for us and for his other creatures and who created the universe as our home. Nature is inconsistent with such a fantasy.

THE REVERSE PROBLEM

No discussion of the question of evil is really complete until it considers one additional issue – one that, given all of the arguments presented so far, most readers would probably never expect. For, according to such philosophers as Peter Kreeft,[105] William Lane Craig,[106] and many others, evil is actually, and rather surprisingly, proof *of* the existence of God. The reason is simple. In their opinion, an atheist who appeals to the problem of evil contradicts himself. By admitting the reality of evil, they say, the atheist has already conceded the point. And they maintain this because they believe that in a godless universe nothing can count as morally good or bad. That is, morality cannot exist without God. But if nothing is good or bad, then there is no evil. If on the other hand there *is* evil, then there must be a God. This argument therefore essentially turns the entire problem on its head.

This idea is somewhat reminiscent of one that we have already encountered. As mentioned above, there are some who respond to the atheist by denying the existence of evil altogether – that is, by denying the reality of misery and suffering (and we've already seen why their solution fails). This new claim is, however, different in several important respects. It does not deny the existence of evil, but instead states that there would be no evil *if* there were no God. Nor is the existence of misery and suffering being questioned. Instead, the claim is that these things could not be *regarded as* bad in the absence of God. This theist objection is therefore entirely new, and must be answered in a completely different way.

The answer to it will be found in the next chapter. For this "reverse problem of evil," as I'm calling it, is an instance of a more general argument, one which may be called the moral argument for the existence of God – and that is the subject to which we now turn.

5

MORALITY

The question I get asked by religious people all the time is, without God, what's to stop me from raping all I want? And my answer is: I do rape all I want. And the amount I want is zero.

— Penn Jillette

Many theists believe that God and morality are closely linked. Some, as has already been mentioned, maintain that atheists cannot be trusted to do the right thing – they suppose, in other words, that belief in God is necessary for leading a morally good life. Fortunately, that opinion is not quite as common as it once was (even if more than half of Americans still think this way). There is, however, another opinion that is more commonly defended by religious thinkers: the idea that without God there can be no *justification* for being moral. Atheists, on this second view, have no basis for being decent and virtuous. It is not that they are necessarily bad. They may accept most of the moral principles that the religious approve of, and may behave just as well. Like theists, they say that murder and rape are reprehensible. But they cannot justify such claims. They do not have a valid reason for adhering to their own principles.

According to this way of thinking, the atheist who refrains from killing, stealing, or even from so much as telling a lie, has been influenced by the standards of society — standards that ultimately derive from God. Like everyone else, the atheist also has self-interested motives to avoid certain forms of behavior, of course: criminal acts might land him in jail, while lesser transgressions might turn him into a social outcast. But in the absence of God, he should have no qualms about doing any of these things *so long as he can get away with them.* There are even a few nonbelievers who seem to agree: the French existentialist Jean-Paul Sartre, for instance — approving of the philosophy expressed by Ivan in *The Brothers Karamazov* — famously declared that "everything is permissible if God does not exist."[107]

A believer who argues in such a way is charging the virtuous atheist with inconsistency. She may also be sounding a warning: if belief in God is needed as a basis for morality, then atheism may eventually lead to the breakdown of standards — and in that case, atheists might just turn into the kind of unscrupulous individuals that they are sometimes accused of being. The main purpose of the argument, however, is to support the existence of God. On this view, nothing would be right or wrong if there were no God. But, the believer goes on to say, some things really *are* right and others really are wrong: after all, isn't it obvious that one should not kill or steal, as well as that one should be kind to others and help those in need? It follows that there must be a God. The "reverse problem of evil" introduced at the end of the previous chapter is one version of this argument: without God, nothing would qualify as evil; since there is evil, there is a God.

COMPETING VIEWS

This argument for the existence of God – which I will refer to as the moral argument – assumes the truth of *ethical objectivism*, the view that there are moral facts which are universally applicable – that, in other words, there are truths regarding right and wrong, and they are the same for everyone. To many, this idea appears indispensable. Without it, they fear, society would collapse into chaos. It is even sometimes claimed that many of the crises facing the modern world are the direct result of a lack of belief in moral truth. Higher divorce rates, drug abuse, increasing violence, stem cell research – all of these things can be blamed on the decline of objectivism. And it is not just the religious who feel this way. Even though it is often claimed that universal moral truths cannot exist in the absence of God, many nonbelievers, as it turns out, are objectivists as well. The new atheist Sam Harris is one example. His recent work *The Moral Landscape* is a book-length defense of the existence of universal values. Harris sees the rejection of objectivism as the source of a number of bad policies on the part of liberal secularists. As he puts it, "Multiculturalism, moral relativism, political correctness, tolerance even of *intolerance* – these are the familiar consequences of separating facts and values on the left."[108]

Many objectivists – theists and nontheists alike – seem to think that the only alternative to their theory is *relativism*. However, there is a third main alternative available. Relativism is the view that there are moral facts, only they are not universal: they vary from place to place and from one era to another. The other theory one can adopt is what is popularly called *subjectivism*. Unlike both objectivism and relativism, subjectivism states that there are no moral facts at all.

An example will clarify the nature of each of these three positions. Consider a moral judgment such as "polygamy is wrong." According to an objectivist, this judgment is either factually correct or factually incorrect.[*] We may not know which is the case, and may therefore disagree with one another over the issue, but the truth is nevertheless "out there," waiting to be discovered. And of course the same thing goes for any other statement in ethics. On the objectivist view, then, there are moral truths, just as there are scientific and mathematical ones. And, as with these others, moral truths are the same for everyone. People may have different *opinions* about them, just as they may have different opinions on scientific matters, but that simply means that some people are right and others wrong. Anyone who maintains that, say, the earth isn't round is *factually* mistaken; so presumably is anyone who maintains that killing an innocent person is okay.

According to a relativist, on the other hand, "polygamy is wrong" is true for some but false for others. Relativism is a common view among secularists, and – as every philosophy instructor knows – is very popular with college students. Allan Bloom even begins his book *The Closing of*

---

[*] This is somewhat simplified for purposes of illustration – a statement like "polygamy is wrong" may be in need of certain qualifications before it can be regarded as either definitely true or definitely false. That is, it could be true in some circumstances and false in others. But we can ignore such details here.

the American Mind by noting – admittedly with a bit of hyperbole – that "one thing a professor can be absolutely certain of" is the relativism of "almost every student entering the university."[109] To truly understand relativism, however, it is important to distinguish between it and a trivial sense in which morality depends on culture. The trivial sense is this: the moral views *held* by one culture are often different from those held by another. For example, in some societies polygamy is regarded as wrong, whereas in others it is allowed. Everyone should acknowledge this much. The ethical relativist goes beyond this initial observation, however, and claims that what is *actually right or wrong* varies from culture to culture. In other words, polygamy really is okay in some places and not okay in others. It is not simply a matter of what people in their respective societies *believe*, but a matter of what the *facts* are. This distinction is often missed because the relativist asserts, in addition, that it is people's beliefs that make some things right and others wrong. Moral principles, according to relativism, are thus nothing over and above the conventions that each society adopts. Nevertheless, they are made *true* by being adopted as the standards of each society; once a particular culture accepts them, they become true for that culture.

Another example that explains the difference between the ethical relativist and one who merely accepts the above kind of "trivial relativism" is this. According to the trivial relativist, it is true that in ancient Rome gladiator contests were *regarded* as acceptable. Romans enjoyed watching people kill each other for sport. But even though they may have found such a thing acceptable, this does not necessarily make it so. It might still be perfectly reasonable for us to condemn the practice, to say such things as "the Romans should not have engaged in that kind of inhumane behavior." An ethical relativist, on the other hand, is one who says "when in Rome..." Or, in other words, according to actual relativism, there was nothing wrong with gladiator sports *back then*. They were not only regarded as acceptable by the Romans, they *were* for that reason acceptable. It would of course be wrong for us to engage in such activities today, since in our society that sort of behavior is no longer allowed. But it wasn't wrong for the Romans to do so.

As to the third view, subjectivism, it says that judgments in ethics are, at root, expressions of our preferences or desires. According to the subjectivist, if I say "polygamy is wrong," I am in fact (whether I realize it or not) essentially expressing my disapproval of it – and probably also attempting to influence others to feel the same way. "Polygamy is wrong" does not, however, describe a fact about the world or about a particular society. In this sense, there are no moral truths or falsehoods. Subjectivism is, of course, compatible with there being individuals who believe that when they are making moral judgments, they are stating facts. The subjectivist claim, in other words, is not that when people say "x is wrong" they always, or even usually, *intend* to do nothing more than express their feelings on the matter. The claim is, rather, that that is what they are in fact doing. Those who believe that they are stating a moral fact when they say "x is wrong" are simply mistaken.

MAIN VIEWS ON THE NATURE OF ETHICS

Objectivism:	There are universal moral facts
Relativism:	There are moral facts, but they are not universal
Subjectivism:	There are no moral facts

As we've seen, proponents of the moral argument suppose that there are universal moral facts, that is, that morality is objective. But in addition – and against non-religious objectivists – they maintain that in order for there to be such facts, there must be a God. A creator is needed in order to properly ground morality. On this view, then, if atheists are correct, either relativism or subjectivism must be true. And the further implication is that without universally binding moral facts, nothing can be properly regarded as good or bad. Neither relativism nor subjectivism is sufficient as a basis for ethics; both eventually lead to nihilism, the idea that where morality is concerned, anything goes. Or so it's claimed.

Very few atheists would agree. Many respond to the theist by asserting that there are objective moral facts even in the absence of God. As already mentioned, Sam Harris is one example. We will consider that kind of answer – including Harris's own version of it – below. Other atheists accept either relativism or subjectivism. They may do so because they agree that there cannot be objective morality without God, or they may argue that there aren't any objective moral principles *but that this has nothing to do with God*. The latter is the position I take. The non-objectivity of ethics has to do with the nature of ethics itself, irrespective of whether or not God exists. Of course, those of us who maintain that there are no objective moral principles usually argue that we don't need them anyway.

The specific theory I support is subjectivism, a much misunderstood and much maligned view. I think that, whereas relativism (just as its critics claim) has problematic implications, the same thing cannot be said of subjectivism – at least not when it is correctly interpreted.

For even though these two theories are often confused with one another, they are very different. Moreover, subjectivism does not mean that we cannot have strong moral values. A subjectivist can in fact take morality very seriously – in some ways, as will be shown below, more seriously even than an objectivist.

In what follows, I criticize the views of theists who maintain that God is necessary for morality as well as some views common among atheists before defending subjectivism. It is important, in my opinion, to point out where many nonbelievers go wrong about the actual nature of ethics. If we leave it to the theists to do so, they may succeed in creating the impression that atheists are incapable of upholding moral principles. Furthermore, only once a correct understanding of this entire issue is achieved can a proper reply be made to the moral argument for the existence of God.

GOD AND MORALITY

The belief that morality is directly dependent on God is based on the divine command theory, an old and controversial view regarding the basis of ethics. Its essential idea is that God issues commands – or at least that he desires certain things to be the case – and that that's what makes some things right and others wrong. Hence, murder and theft are immoral because he prohibited them, whereas loving one's neighbors and respecting one's parents are right because he commanded those. To the average religious person, this theory probably sounds correct. It may even appear obvious. But it is a view riddled with difficulties, and one that has been rejected not only by nonbelievers but by many religious thinkers as well.

On the divine command theory, the only thing that makes something right or wrong, good or bad, is that God says so. It's important to distinguish this view from one in which God merely *informs* us regarding what is right or wrong. If God tells us not to kill *because he knows that killing is wrong*, then the wrongness of killing logically precedes God's decision to tell us: killing was already wrong, and would have been wrong even if God had not told us that it was. By contrast, the divine command theory states that, had God not decided to regard murder in such a negative way, then it would *not* have been wrong. That may already give the reader some pause. Even worse, if God commanded the opposite – if he told us to kill one another and really hate our neighbor's guts – then *those* things would be good. It is for this reason that Gottfried Leibniz, the great 18th-century polymath, complained that the divine command theory "destroys, without realizing it, all the love of God and all his glory; for why praise him for what he has done, if he would be equally praiseworthy in doing the contrary?"[110]

Of course one might at this point object that God would never command such things as murder and hatred.* The divine command theorist must be careful here, however. It may be the case that God would never command such things, but not because they are bad. Remember: they wouldn't be bad if God did command them! Any theist who claims that murder is bad, and that *for that reason* God would never want us to kill one another, is in effect admitting that something other than God's wishes makes it bad. And that is inconsistent with the theory. Therefore,

---

* Though in fact, if one is referring to the biblical God, he *did* command some of us to kill others, as we've already seen. But we can ignore such complications for now.

the fact that something is bad cannot be the reason God forbids it – nor the fact that something is good be the reason he commands it. On the divine command theory, he cannot command or prohibit anything at all for *moral* reasons. His commands are therefore morally arbitrary. As far as ethics is concerned, God might as well flip a coin.

It could be, however, that God's *nature* is such that he would not, in fact, command murder, or any of the other things that we normally think of as wrong. God may just be a loving being. He desires us to be nice to one another rather than, say, viciously harm one another. And to say that God is loving is not necessarily to evaluate him as good (and therefore does not introduce an independent standard of goodness that the theory cannot explain). In fact, one can imagine an individual – for instance, Attila the Hun – who might disapprove of God's loving nature, and hence call it bad. To say that God is loving, then, is not to morally praise God, but rather to describe a characteristic he supposedly has: God likes kindness and dislikes suffering. Therefore, he commands us to help the poor, comfort the sick, and all the rest. And that may seem to solve the problem.

It doesn't. For now the question that's raised is whether it is God's loving nature that makes his commands good. That is, either the commands are good because of his loving nature or they would be good even if his nature were different. Now, if God's commands would still be good were he not loving, then we haven't solved the problem – for in that case, it would still be true that if God *were* to command murder, murder would be good. But if, on the other hand, the argument is that God's commands are good *because* he is loving, then this does introduce an independent standard of goodness. And then the argument for the necessity of God falls apart, for in this case there is a separate reason for something being good. An easy way to understand the difficulty is this: if God's commands are good because he is loving, then it follows that what is essential for goodness is *being in accordance with the desires of one who is loving.* So long, in other words, as a moral judgment is in keeping with what a loving being would want, it is right. But a theist who claims this can no longer consistently claim that without God nothing would count as good or bad. Anything that is in accordance with what such a loving being would desire, *irrespective of whether or not this being exists*, would be good. Such a modification of the theory therefore makes it incompatible with the moral argument for the existence of God. A creator is no longer indispensable for morality.

It seems clear that the divine command theory does not work. But no theist should be disturbed by such a conclusion, for any view that makes morality directly dependent on God leads to results that most find completely unacceptable anyway. To see this, suppose you believe that without a supreme being there is no right or wrong. And now imagine that tomorrow you become convinced that God does not exist after all. Do you really think you would suddenly regard, say, torturing babies as a perfectly reasonable hobby for anyone who happens to enjoy it? I sincerely hope not. Nor do I think any sane person would. But that is exactly what the theory asks us to accept. Remember, torturing babies, according to this theory, is not wrong because it causes pain and misery, violates individual rights, or anything else of the sort; it is wrong only because God says so. If there is no God, it is perfectly okay. The situation here can also be represented by a thought experiment in which there are two possible universes, exactly alike in every respect except that one is created by God and the other isn't; and where in the first an action that causes needless and terrible suffering is wrong, while in the second that very same action is just fine. But why should the presence or absence of a deity make such a difference – or *any* difference at all?

A theist can avoid all of these problems (though not *all* problems, as we'll see) by defending the other main possibility: that certain actions are simply right and others simply wrong, and that God, when he issues his commands, does so in accordance with what the moral facts are. Or, in other words, that God merely reveals to us what is right and what is wrong. But notice that on such a view, if there is no God but everything else remains unchanged, then the same moral principles still apply. In the two-universes thought experiment that was just mentioned, morality is the same in both. And in that case, the above argument for the existence of God no longer works. It also follows that nonbelievers can be every bit as justified in regarding what is right as right and what is wrong as wrong – or, in other words, that belief in God is unnecessary as a basis for morality. One possible reply to the moral argument for the existence of God, then, is that there are moral facts which exist in their own right. Many nonbelievers, as I've said, hold this view. In the next section I consider their position.

Anyone holding that there are objective moral principles existing independently of God must still explain the origin or basis of those principles, however. And as we'll see, that's not an easy thing to do. This suggests that perhaps we haven't yet arrived at the correct reply to the moral argument.

The thesis that God is necessary for ethics is not based exclusively on the idea that God is the source of moral value. It also has its roots in the suspicion that in a completely natural world – one devoid of a supernatural agency of any kind – there is no room for objective right or wrong. A merely physical, impersonal universe is utterly indifferent to our concerns and existence. How could objective moral truth be part of such a world? The proponent of the moral argument can therefore turn the tables around at this point and go on the offensive. Perhaps ethics has not been shown to be dependent on God. But can the atheist do any better? In a godless world, what is the source of values? Christian philosopher Chad Meister put the problem this way:

> Did the big bang somehow spew forth moral platitudes like "Be compassionate to others," "Care for those in need" and "Love your enemies"? If not, where did they come from? What makes them something more than mere subjective opinions?[111]

When faced with an argument like Meister's, many atheists turn to evolutionary explanations. Natural selection can tell us, they say, why we human beings behave as we do, including why we perform acts of altruism. And that's certainly true: Darwin's theory can account for all of that. The only problem is that that's not an answer to the theist's challenge. It does not address the issue of where *right* and *wrong* themselves come from.

A description of our moral behavior in terms of evolutionary theory does provide us with a reply to another frequent theistic complaint. There are those who maintain that science by itself cannot explain the development of selflessness and compassion, and who therefore suppose that these things must come from God.[112] Consider, for instance, the fact that many of us are at times motivated to help starving people halfway across the world. Why should that be? That sort of behavior does not appear to be in any way conducive to our own reproductive success, and therefore should not have been picked up if our psychological attributes are the result of natural selection. Remember, according to Darwin, it is the characteristics (including the behavioral traits) of the individuals who leave the most offspring that end up in the gene pool. Therefore, behaviors that are not useful to the continuation of an individual's genetic line are weeded out. So why is it that we care about starving children in the Sudan? How does that help us pass our genes along?

It is easy enough to understand caring about one's relatives: they share much of our genetic material, after all. Support given to family members helps ensure that some of our genes survive. Nor is it difficult to account for generous behavior toward those who are our friends and acquaintances. It can be explained in terms of the "you scratch my back, I'll scratch yours" strategy. Individuals benefit by the assistance of others, and yet others are only going to assist you if you are nice to them too. In fact, this so-called "reciprocal altruism" is not at all uncommon throughout the animal kingdom. Much of it even occurs between different species, where it goes by the name "symbiosis." (It is important to realize that although all this is based on what nature selected for, and thus ultimately depends on what is in a sense advantageous for us, it does not follow that the resulting behavior is selfish. It is not as if a person does something for another only in the hope of getting something in return. Much less is it the case that a mother cares for her children solely because she wants her genetic line to continue! To think so is to completely misunderstand the Darwinian account. The idea, rather, is that human beings developed certain feelings toward others because it was genetically beneficial for them to do so. The feelings are nonetheless quite genuine.) But all this still leaves us with a puzzle regarding kindness toward complete strangers, especially in the context of a large modern city, or toward those living in distant places, for it is not likely that such acts will ever be repaid. Why aren't our sympathies limited to those whom we know?

A big part of the answer lies in the fact that the characteristics our species acquired were the ones that made us successful, not in our current environment, but in what is known as our "ancestral environment." Our ancestors lived in small, relatively isolated tribal groups, where they rarely came into contact with strangers. It was to deal with situations usually found in that kind of setting that we developed our moral sentiments. Under those circumstances, all of the individuals we helped were likely to respond in kind. Moreover, cooperation was essential for survival. But then something unexpected happened: civilization was invented. This is not a development that natural selection could have foreseen – natural selection has no predictive powers whatsoever. As a result, our moral sentiments toward non-relatives, originally evolved for the purpose of providing us with reciprocal altruism and with the cooperation of tribal members, are now also applied to individuals who cannot return the favor.

This change is only partial, of course. People still care more about those nearer them than those very far away, and residents of large cities are notoriously less friendly toward strangers than those of small towns. And it is still ongoing: the more we are exposed to those from distant places, the less narrow-minded we tend to be. This is related to one of the problems with religious morality. The ethical principles found in such works as the Bible and the Koran are those of a more tribalistic age. That is why they are filled with injunctions to kill outsiders (as we have already seen with regards to the Bible) and why many of their seemingly more enlightened moral precepts are not what they appear to be: the commands to love your neighbor as yourself and to refrain from killing others were originally meant to apply only within the tribe; those outside the group didn't really matter. Even Jesus, by his own admission, came exclusively for "the lost sheep of the house of Israel," and regarded gentiles as mere dogs.[113] Christians may be convinced that Jesus loves them, but he clearly does not. The problem with holding on to old-time religion, then, is that it prevents us from escaping this in-group mentality; it delays the kind of moral progress that is being discussed here.

In spite of religion, however, there has in fact been much progress of this kind. And though the complete story is undoubtedly more complex, and other factors are almost certainly involved, we nevertheless have here the basis for a scientific explanation of the fact that we are moral beings who often care for others. God isn't needed. But once again, this has nothing to do with the issue of objectivity. That there are ways to account for our moral sentiments by invoking natural selection provides us with a way to understand why those sentiments exist; it does not show that those sentiments are factually correct. The evolutionary explanation is in fact compatible with there being no objective moral truths at all. In order to draw the further conclusion that evolutionary ethics gives us a basis for objective morality, one must accept the additional premise that natural selection is in some way tied to moral truth. And that's where the difficulty lies.

Still, the idea that evolutionary explanations can supply us with objective answers regarding right and wrong is not without its defenders. In his 1879 work *Data of Ethics*, Herbert Spencer – the philosopher who coined the phrase "survival of the fittest" – argued that right conduct is conduct that produces what is, from the standpoint of evolution, beneficial. The goal of proper behavior, on this view, is to prolong life, increase its quality, and produce more offspring – and that, according to Spencer, is best achieved when human beings organize themselves into harmonious communities in which they can work together for their mutual benefit. Peaceful, cooperative behavior is therefore objectively good behavior. But such a theory – even if its ultimate conclusion seems acceptable to many – is highly suspect at best. After all, why is it necessarily good to pursue what biology dictates? If we really believed that, we would all have as many children as possible.

Another objectivist theory is the utilitarian one defended by new atheist Sam Harris. Whereas for Spencer what is good is what is conducible to our biological success, for Harris the good is identified with the well-being of conscious creatures, and morality is exclusively concerned with increasing the overall amount of that quality. Harris is somewhat clearer than Spencer, so I'll concentrate on his views. Unlike the latter, Harris specifically states that moral terms *mean the same thing* as certain non-moral equivalents. Thus for example, in a blog post clarifying his argument, he wrote:

> "You shouldn't lie" (prescriptive) is syn-
> onymous with "Lying needlessly com-
> plicates people's lives, destroys reputations,

and undermines trust" (descriptive). "We should defend democracy from total-itarianism" (prescriptive) is another way of saying "Democracy is far more conducive to human flourishing than the alternatives are" (descriptive).[114]

Harris has also implied that "good" is synonymous with "the well-being of conscious creatures," and made analogous statements regarding other evaluative concepts. The problem is that, as the philosopher G. E. Moore demonstrated over one hundred years ago, views of this type – those that claim moral terms are identical in meaning to some non-moral description – commit a basic error. The simple fact is that that is not how moral terms are used.

If "good" were synonymous with "well-being," it would make no sense to ask whether some action that increases well-being is really good. It would be like asking whether an action that increases *good* is really good. But in fact, one can meaningfully ask such a question about well-being, as will be shown below. Similarly, one can meaningfully ask whether one should lie in spite of the consequences of dishonesty, or whether democracy should be defended because it is the political system most conducive to human flourishing – or, for that matter (to return to Spencer for a moment), whether some action that is beneficial to our species is the right one to pursue.

Harris's argument has convinced quite a few people, however, and I think in part this is due to its initial plausibility: it just seems obvious to many that increasing the total amount of well-being in the world *has* to be the right thing to do. In fact, this appears so obvious to Harris that he simply denies the Moorean objection: "it makes no sense at all," he replies, "to ask whether maximizing well-being is 'good'."[115] But though his view may appear convincing at first, like other forms of utilitarianism it leads to conclusions that most of us find decidedly un-reasonable. The problem arises because the view treats well-being as the *only* good, and therefore as the sole feature worth considering. As a result, it ignores other important factors, including matters of justice or rights.

In his classic work *Anarchy, State, and Utopia*, the philosopher Robert Nozick asked his readers to imagine alien beings "who would get enormously greater life satisfaction from devouring us than we would lose."[116] If such creatures existed, our becoming their dinner would, according to Harris's theory, be a good thing, for it would increase the overall amount of well-being in the universe: the satisfaction that these creatures would gain would exceed any loss on our part. It seems that we should therefore sacrifice ourselves for their benefit – an obvious refutation of utilitarianism as far as most people are concerned. Always maximizing well-being only sounds good until you realize that one creature's happiness may come at the expense of another's – and even of another creature's very existence. This is where such important things as freedom and equality need to be taken into account. Without them, one might have to say that it could be good for every human being on earth to be devoured by gruesome aliens.

You might suppose Harris would try to argue his way out of such an unpalatable conclusion. Not so. Here's what he says:

> Nozick... asks if it would be ethical for our species to be sacrificed for the unim-aginably vast happiness of some super-

beings. Provided that we take the time to really imagine the details (which is not easy), I think the answer is clearly "yes." There seems to be no reason to suppose that we must occupy the highest peak on the moral landscape. If there are beings who stand in relation to us as we do to bacteria, it should be easy to admit that their interests must trump our own... I do not think that the existence of such a moral hierarchy poses any problems for our ethics.[117]

At least Harris must be praised for his consistency. But I wonder if he would willingly walk into the aliens' spaceship, to be taken away to the slaughterhouse, as in the classic *Twilight Zone* episode "To Serve Man." Should parents allow their children to be sacrificed as well? Most of us would say that the answer to Nozick's thought experiment is not clearly yes at all, but clearly no.

Nor do we have to have to depend on such "science-fictiony" examples to make this point. Suppose a surgeon has five patients who immediately need organ transplants, plus one healthy one (who perhaps came in for a minor procedure) who is a match for the others. No organs are otherwise available. Should the surgeon kill the healthy patient to save the other five? After all, everything else being equal, saving five lives at the expense of one would increase the overall amount of well-being in the world.

When faced with this challenge, some utilitarians point out that if such things were common practice no one would trust the medical profession, and as a result well-being would in fact decrease. But what if this were a one-time occurrence – one in which the surgeon in question managed to make the death of the healthy patient appear accidental? Would it then be a good thing? Not according to the vast majority of people, and I hope not according to you. It is wrong to intentionally kill an innocent person, even in order to save five others. One thing this example shows is that utilitarianism is too simple a theory to capture what most of us regard as important in ethics. But more importantly for our discussion, what it also shows is that Harris's contention that an increase in well-being is necessarily good can reasonably be disputed. At the very least, it *makes sense* to ask whether killing an innocent person in order to save five is a good thing, even if doing so would undoubtedly increase the total amount of well-being. And that refutes Harris's view. "Good" cannot mean the same thing as "well-being." If it did, it wouldn't even make sense to question whether killing the one person would be good.

Not all attempts to defend moral objectivism without appealing to God commit the same error, of course. But, even though it would be beyond the scope of this book to consider every way such a thing has been attempted, it does appear that all of them are in one way or another problematic. To take just one example: one form of objectivism that is very different from Harris's is called intuitionism, and (unlike the theories we have discussed so far) it does not claim that moral properties, like goodness, are equivalent to some non-moral properties, like well-being or what is beneficial to our species. Rather, it maintains that *in addition* to non-moral properties, there are moral ones that certain things or states-of-affair possess. So for example, an act of kindness, besides containing other properties, contains the moral property of goodness. This property cannot be observed, like physical ones can, but is instead known to us by means of our moral intuition – hence the name of the theory. The problem, though, is that there appears to be no reason to postulate such mysterious properties when we can easily and reasonably explain the existence of our moral sentiments without them. And, as we will see below, that is exactly what subjectivism does.

It appears, then, that atheists have failed to show that moral truths exist in a godless world. This shouldn't be seen as a victory for theism, however. The fact is that the above considerations apply to believer and nonbeliever alike. Atheists may be unable to account for the objectivity of ethics, but not because of anything having to do with their atheism. Believers are just as incapable of defending the truth of moral principles. After all, they must either claim that moral truths are dependent on God, in which case they run into the problems already discussed; or claim that moral principles exist in their own right, in which case they run into the same problems as an atheist: how to find objective principles in the world out there. The proponents of the moral argument, then, have no real reason to be satisfied by anything that's been said so far.

If moral objectivism cannot be defended, that only leaves relativism and subjectivism. And of the two, the more popular by far is relativism – a theory that in the opinion of its followers is not only unproblematic, but is the one view that is both reasonable *and admirable*. It is, they believe, the tolerant alternative to the kind of closed-minded universalism most people embrace. We must therefore consider this view before proceeding to our final theory.

WHY NOT RELATIVISM?

In 1996, a seventeen-year-old girl named Fauziya Kazinga fled her native country of Togo to seek asylum in the United States so as to avoid undergoing female circumcision, a painful and dangerous procedure still performed in several places around the world. Because this was a rather newsworthy event, the attorney representing her, Karen Musalo, was interviewed by the news media on several occasions. Now, you might expect that people here, in a land where female circumcision is neither practiced nor permitted, would pretty much all be in agreement with the idea of protecting this girl. And indeed she was eventually granted asylum. Musalo, however, reports that as her attorney, she was repeatedly asked what right she had "to judge or condemn the cultural practices" of a different society. "I was sometimes accused of being a 'cultural imperialist' by imposing my Western concept of human rights on a very different culture..."[118] Musalo was attacked for daring to suggest that certain foreign customs were unacceptable. In the opinion of her critics, any disapproval of a different way of life is apparently forbidden; it is closed-minded prejudice. Tolerance demands that we respect other cultures, and this means not criticizing them.

This, however, is tolerance taken much too far – and it is something these critics would never have believed were it not for the prevalence of relativism in our society. It all starts out innocently enough. Individuals who are more open-minded tend to regard the moral differences of other cultures less critically. If in another country a woman is allowed to go topless in public, or the eating of beans is considered a sin, or some such thing, who are we to tell them they are wrong? We do things our way, they do it theirs. However, such open-mindedness encourages some to think of ethics as applying only locally. On such a view, our principles are the more-or-less arbitrary customs adopted by us, just as their principles are the ones adopted by them – and we cannot use the standards of one society to judge those of another. Now, all this might sound fine as long as the issue is breasts or beans; but when it is, say, the sacrifice of a child on an altar or the burning of a widow on her husband's funeral pyre, it becomes much more troubling. Most people wouldn't go so far as to view such practices as nothing more than "a different way of doing things." A convinced relativist might, however. Relativism, in other words, creates in its adherents an extreme reluctance to criticize the customs of other peoples, no matter how vile those customs may be. It leads to acquiescence with respect to practices that, if conducted next door, would be treated as inadmissible. And it is precisely this that concerns many opponents of the theory.

The above is a moral complaint to relativism, and of course there are those who may not be troubled by it: anyone who feels that we should not interfere with other cultures, not even if it is the only way to protect innocent lives, won't be convinced by any of what's been said so far. But there are other ways of criticizing the theory. It suffers from conceptual difficulties as well.

Relativists never seem to notice the tension between advocating relativism on the one hand, and urging tolerance as if it's a *universal* moral principle on the other, but there is in fact a deep problem here. Looked at one way, the theory says that, since the moral principles adopted by other peoples are "true for them," they cannot be criticized using principles that are merely "true for us." Each society's ideals apply only within that society. This is of course the source of its exaggerated emphasis on tolerance. Looked at another way, however, such open-mindedness toward foreign customs isn't really a logical consequence of the theory at all. For what is right in a culture is what is held to be right within that culture – and that of course includes the level of tolerance of other societies deemed appropriate. Thus, according to this second way of looking at it, relativists should not automatically embrace unlimited tolerance after all. They should instead adopt whatever the norm is in their own society. To put it another way, it may be that, by the standards of their own theory, it is relativists themselves who are committing a moral wrong by being too open-minded.

A related difficulty is that relativists do not really believe that their moral views are right only because they are the views accepted by the society they find themselves in. If they really believed that, they would form their moral opinions based on what society as a whole accepts, and would be ready to change these opinions whenever they clashed with the prevailing views. Since neither of these is the case, relativists are in fact inconsistent with their own principles.

I think that if these problems were widely recognized they would put an end to relativism. It is a popular theory only because it is misunderstood by its own proponents. When one looks at it more closely, it in fact seems the least defensible of all the theories on the nature of ethics.

With both objectivism and relativism out of the way, we can now move on to subjectivism. However, if one is going to defend this view, one must be careful to state precisely what it means, for subjectivism tends to be misunderstood – and when that happens, it can lead to even worse consequences than the ones we have just discussed.

Theories are often misinterpreted. Perhaps the best-known example of this is how in the late 19th Century the theory of evolution led to a movement known as social Darwinism. Its proponents advanced a rather distorted view of Darwin's ideas and proceeded to apply it to the moral and political issues of the day.* An even more ridiculous and more amusing example of misinterpretation involves the theory of relativity and its effect on certain fashionable pseudo-intellectuals of the Jazz Age. As historian Paul Johnson explains, with the popularization of Einstein's ideas after they were dramatically confirmed during a solar eclipse in 1919, "the belief began to circulate...that there were no longer any absolutes: of time and space, of good and evil, of knowledge, above all of value. Mistakenly but perhaps inevitably, relativity became confused with relativism."[119] Einstein's theory, needless to say, has nothing whatsoever to do with the nature of ethics.

Subjectivism, too, is open to misunderstanding and misrepresentation. It is often identified with the view that, where morality is concerned, anything goes. After all, if there are no facts about right and wrong, what reason is there for doing one thing as opposed to another? Why care about anything at all? Proponents of the moral argument for the existence of God in particular tend to make this claim. As they see it, subjectivism means that everyone can do exactly as he or she pleases: armed robbery, murder, arson, and even homosexual marriage

---

* Herbert Spencer is usually counted among them, though his views were somewhat more sophisticated than those of most social Darwinists.

are the potential end results. And other ethical objectivists usually agree. But in fact subjectivism implies no such thing.

According to subjectivism, moral judgments are the expressions of certain of our preferences or desires. There is more to be said about such judgments, of course, since not all of our attitudes qualify as moral; a complete account would have to spell out what makes morality particularly important for us and why it is set apart from other concerns. But that's not essential for our present purposes. It is enough for us to note that we feel certain ways about certain things and that at least some of these we take very seriously. Our views about right and wrong are the direct result of such feelings. Moreover, although not everyone feels the same way about moral issues, there is nevertheless a great deal of intersubjective agreement. Just about everyone regards theft as wrong, for instance (*all* of us, in fact, provided we are the victim). Even those who steal often rationalize their actions in order to assure themselves that, in their particular case, what they are doing isn't "really" wrong (think of people who take ashtrays from hotel rooms with the excuse that, after all, the hotelier expects this sort of thing and thus takes it into account when calculating rates). Ethical objectivists notice this intersubjective agreement and conclude that there must be a moral reality "out there" which we somehow detect. Subjectivists simply eliminate that moral reality as superfluous. The level of agreement among individuals is a result of our common evolved human nature, along with the social conditioning that builds upon that nature. The fact that we have certain feelings of approval and disapproval is sufficient to explain what we observe. And of course that we have such feelings does not imply that they are "factually correct." The question of correctness does not even arise. Feelings, unlike beliefs, aren't true or false.

The reality of our feelings is also sufficient to dismiss the notion that subjectivism reduces to nihilism – that, in other words, it leads to moral anarchy. Nihilism, as I'm using the term here, is a moral position, a point of view as to what should be done (and a very unusual one at that); it is not – like objectivism, relativism, and subjectivism – a theory about the nature of ethics. It does not attempt to answer the question "what is morality based on?" but rather the question "what ought one to do?" And it answers it with "anyone can do whatever they feel like doing," which is what makes it such a problematic, amoral view. It is actually rather easy to demonstrate that nihilism does not follow from subjectivism, however. Someone who claims that it does follow is arguing one of two things: either that subjectivism entails that *it is true* that everything is morally permissible; or else that it entails that *as a matter of everyone's subjective opinion*, without moral facts everything becomes permissible. But the first obviously cannot be, since according to subjectivism there are no moral truths! And the second is the opinion of only a very small number of individuals; the great majority of subjectivists, like the great majority of other people, do not hold such a view. Subjectivism therefore does not imply nihilism. It merely states that moral judgments are rooted in our feelings – and since we regard our feelings in these matters as important, we can be subjectivists and continue to think of morality as very serious business. Once one understands that truth has nothing to do with it – once one sees that it is entirely beside the point – its absence becomes irrelevant.

A related concern is that, given subjectivism, there is no basis for condemning anyone, no matter how vile. One common complaint is that you cannot even prove that Hitler was wrong – it's merely your subjective opinion, which just happens to be different from some other people's opinion. And in fact it is correct that one cannot *prove* anything of a purely moral nature: there is nothing to prove, after all, if there are no moral truths. But again, so what? It doesn't follow that our opinions shouldn't matter to us. Moreover, others can certainly be condemned on the basis of these opinions. Criminals disagree with the majority of us as to what one can and cannot do, and thus the majority, as a society, condemns and punishes them. Provided you agree with society and not with the criminals, you should have no complaints.

Perhaps another concern is that, without some factual grounds, one has no conclusive means by which to change someone else's mind. Does supposing there are moral truths really help in that regard, however? Imagine a debate between two ethical objectivists, say, between Harris and Spencer over the question of the afore-mentioned alien superbeings who want to devour us. Harris thinks the human race should be sacrificed to these beings; Spencer thinks it should not. I'm sure they could argue the point until the superbeings starve to death and still find no resolution. That they both think their own views are true makes no difference whatsoever. It does not help them resolve their differences. Nor does the fact that I think my own view on the issue is a subjective preference make me feel any less strongly in its favor.

It is also common to suppose – and the above may very well appear to suggest – that subjectivism rules out reasoned moral debate. But once again that is not the case. In the first place, much of what is considered moral debate actually concerns *facts* surrounding the issues in question. Consider two individuals holding opposing views on capital punishment. Perhaps one supports it because he believes that capital punishment works as a deterrent, whereas the other denies this and thus opposes it. Now, whether or not capital punishment is a deterrent to crime is a factual question. If that is what the disagreement is fundamentally about, then there is in principle a simple way to resolve it: find out what the truth is about deterrence. (Of course, in practice things are almost never this simple or straightforward. Many people, even after being presented with conclusive evidence against a view that they hold, simply refuse to budge. My point, however, is that it is possible *in principle* to resolve disputes this way.) So at least that sort of thing is perfectly compatible with subjectivism. But in the second place, even where debate is of a purely moral nature – in other words, even when two people agree on all the facts and still disagree over what is the right thing to do – there is room for reasoned argument. Our moral principles may be ultimately nothing more than subjective preferences, but still, we want to have a *coherent set* of such preferences. We cannot act in a consistent manner unless that is the case, for otherwise we would be pulled in different directions by our various competing desires. And so, even when it comes to purely moral disagreement, there are issues that can be raised and discussed. Nor is it hard to see how this works. For instance, there are many individuals who, on first encountering it, find utilitarianism appealing: the only thing we need be concerned about, they imagine, is increasing the overall amount of happiness or well-being in the world. Since everyone desires happiness, such a theory may initially sound perfectly reasonable. But once it is pointed out that one of its implications is that the human race ought to be sacrificed to Nozick's hypothetical superbeings, the majority of people change their minds. That is, once they see that in order to apply the principles of utilitarianism consistently they also have to accept conclusions that they cannot agree with, they reconsider. Of course there are those, like Harris, who stick to their guns, but that just means that they are attempting to adopt a different set of internally consistent principles. And supposing that the principles in question are objective makes no difference here. As already pointed out, it does not help people resolve their differences.

Even after hearing the above sort of explanations, many people remain skeptical of subjectivism. The theory doesn't satisfy them because it just doesn't seem sufficiently "solid." There is a tendency to suppose that, if moral principles are not rooted in fact, then they cannot really matter. If it isn't *true* that, say, torturing puppies is bad, then why not just go ahead and do it? But to make such a claim is to assume that only facts that are independent of us are important. And why should that be? We – the great majority of us, at any rate – are extremely opposed to torturing puppies. It's something we simply would never condone. That means we *do* regard it as important: it matters to us if someone does such a thing, and we want very much to prevent it. It is actually rather strange to assume that moral principles count only if they are in some sense true. That implies that our feelings about things do not matter *unless some further fact supports them*. But why should that be, and how would such a further fact make a difference anyway? It seems to me that our moral interests are self-supporting; they do not require external justification. I regard my moral views as important, and you regard yours as important. And fortunately, for the most part, our views are probably in agreement, at least in their most fundamental aspects.

That is why, earlier in the book, I was able to criticize Old Testament morality in such a way so as to at least create some doubt in the minds of many believers. It is not because it is "true" that some of that morality is wrong. Rather, it is because the majority of people – including of those who are religious – can't find it in themselves to condone some of the terrible things that Yahweh supposedly approved of. In other words, all people in our society have, as one might expect, approximately the same moral sentiments, at least with regards to certain fundamental issues. And it is rare for someone to stick to their guns when faced with clear evidence that their views lead to intuitively immoral results.

This sort of thing can be seen in a story related by the ex-preacher and atheist Dan Barker. During a debate with Pastor Douglas Wilson, Barker read from Psalm 137:9, which says of the Babylonians, "Happy shall he be, that taketh and dasheth thy little ones against the stones." He then asked Wilson, "Is it moral to throw little babies against rocks?" According to the account, Wilson, with only some hesitation, replied that yes, it is moral. Barker reports that "there was audible gasping from members of the audience,"[120] including from many of the Christians there. Wilson could not bring himself to abandon, or even to question, his strict adherence to God's word – even if that meant saying that murdering babies is okay. But judging from their reaction, the faith of many of those in the audience was, fortunately, not quite as unshakeable as that.

In some ways, subjectivism actually provides a more solid foundation for morality than objectivism does. Most people approve of objectivism because they of course believe that the true moral principles are the ones that they themselves hold. Religious people think moral truth is found in the doctrines of their religion (even if, like members of the above audience, they are sometimes inconsistent about it), and nonbelievers think it is found in whatever secular view they support. But the claim that there is *a* moral truth is of course separable from the claim that this or that is *the* moral truth. It follows that if objectivism is correct – if there is a moral truth – it might not be the one that you hold. Fully informed individuals disagree on what the alleged truth is, and no one has been able to come up with a theory that convinces everyone. But now suppose the correct morality *is* the one found in the Bible – and that it would therefore be moral to throw the babies of ancient Babylonians against rocks. Then, no matter how much it might bother us, we would have to accept that fact. Or suppose Harris *is* right and it is moral to sacrifice the entire human species for the benefit of super-intelligent aliens. Then we ought to voluntarily give them our children to be devoured: after all, it would be the right thing to do. If you are an objectivist, your commitment should be to the truth, no matter what that is – and that means you cannot consider even your most fundamental moral principles as inviolable. A subjectivist, however, does not have this problem. And this means that a subjectivist can actually adhere more firmly to fundamental principles than an objectivist can.

Subjectivism is not the terrible theory that its critics typically take it to be. It nonetheless must be admitted that, since it is often misunderstood, subjectivism might inadvertently lead some people to a nihilistic worldview. That is, there are some individuals who, if they are convinced of the truth of subjectivism, might conclude that as a result they should have no qualms about doing anything whatsoever. And that is a real concern. However, the misrepresentation of the theory by its critics is the main cause of this. Those who insist that subjectivism is equivalent to nihilism might convince some people that nothing they do matters. There is a parallel here between critics of subjectivism and many critics of atheism: those who argue that atheism cannot justify morality might also convince some that, if there is no God, they do not have to be morally responsible. Ironically, then, it is for the most part the critics of these allegedly subversive views that make them potentially dangerous.

SUBJECTIVISM AND EVIL

There remains one apparent difficulty: how can a subjectivist – who after all does not believe in objective values – employ the argument from evil to claim that the suffering and injustice we see all around us is evidence against the existence of God? Isn't the atheistic subjectivist who does so contradicting himself by claiming that there is evil after all? This point was made by, among others, C. S. Lewis in his very popular work, *Mere Christianity*. Lewis, who used to be a nonbeliever before turning into one of the most widely-read defenders of the faith, regarded his former view as confused for exactly this reason:

> My argument against God was that the universe seemed so cruel and unjust. But how had I got this idea of *just* and *unjust*? ... Of course I could have given up my idea of justice by saying it was nothing but a private idea of my own. But if I did that, then my argument against God collapsed too – for the argument depended on saying that the

world was really unjust, not simply that it
did not happen to please my fancies.[121]

(Note, incidentally, Lewis's talent for caricaturing a view he
opposes: a moral principle as viewed by a subjectivist is
characterized as something that just *happens to please his
fancies*. Could he have made subjectivism sound any more
frivolous?)

There are two things a subjectivist can say in reply to
this. First, the problem of evil is primarily an *internal
problem* for the theist who believes in a perfect God. The
issue is not so much whether there really is evil, but
whether the theistic view is internally consistent. Most
theists believe both in a perfect God and in the existence
of evil, and the question is whether both of these things
can be true at the same time. This is something that
theists have debated amongst themselves. A subjectivist,
then, could be interpreted as merely pointing out that the
theist's worldview is self-contradictory, and in order to do
this he does not have to maintain that there is actual evil.

But there is more. The second thing a subjectivist can
argue is that it's not the existence of objective evil that is
significant. It is the existence of suffering and other things
we *regard* as evil that matters. Whether or not such things
are objectively bad is beside the point. If the theist claims
that there is a perfectly good God, she is presumably
claiming that there is a being who does not want there to
be needless suffering or other such things. The term
"good" is, after all, used by the great majority of people in
this way (and if the theist means something else by it – if
she thinks a good God enjoys watching people die in
horrible ways – she should make that clear). It follows
that, if needless suffering and the like do occur, then there
cannot be such a God, and a subjectivist is entirely within

159

his rights in making this claim. It is not in any way connected with the existence of moral facts.

There is one sense in which the abandonment of objectivity in ethics is relevant to the debate between theists and atheists, however. If the theist believes in the perfect God we considered in the previous chapter, she believes in a being that is *defined* as being all good – in other words, his goodness is supposedly a fact about him. One of his supposed properties is moral perfection. If morality is subjective, however, then there are no moral properties, and thus it cannot be a *fact* that God is good. To say that God is morally perfect is, on the subjectivist view, merely to express one's complete approval of God – it is essentially to claim that he has those characteristics that one morally favors over all others. A person with different moral attitudes might agree on what characteristics God has, and yet regard him as bad. To say that God is perfectly good, then, is not to say that he has the *property* of being good; there isn't any such property. It follows that the perfect God, defined as including the property of moral perfection, cannot exist. The concept of such a being is a confused one; it cannot apply to anything. The theist who believes in this God bases her belief upon an erroneous theory about values. Therefore, although as we have already seen one cannot validly argue from moral objectivism to the existence of God, one *can* validly argue in the opposite direction, from subjectivism to the conclusion that there is no God of the type most people believe in.

WHAT ATHEISTS SHOULD SAY ABOUT MORALITY

We began this chapter by asking whether atheism can justify morality. The answer is somewhat complex. First,

160

atheism is not, when contrasted with theism, at a disadvantage on this issue. If one view can provide a justification for our judgments in ethics, so can the other. However, if by "justifying morality" what is meant is providing a factual basis for it, then the conclusion we have reached is that morality cannot be justified by either position. But – and this is the most important point – even if this is true it doesn't follow that morality is unimportant, nor that it should be ignored. If morality is not grounded in fact, then it has no justification in the above sense of the word, but neither does it require one: it is enough that we care about things, that we desire some things to be the case and others not to be the case. That is what in the final analysis matters to us. It is solely on that basis that we disapprove of certain types of behavior while at the same time encouraging others. Nothing else is needed.

The recent documentary film *Collision* (already mentioned in passing back in chapter three) is based on a fascinating series of debates between atheist Christopher Hitchens and the aforementioned Douglas Wilson. The two had previously battled in print and published the results in a small volume entitled *Is Christianity Good for the World?* Both in the movie and in the book, a large part of the disagreement between them concerns the foundation of ethics. As might be expected, Wilson repeatedly affirms that an atheist has no grounds on which to make moral pronouncements. Someone like Hitchens, he says, shouldn't care, for instance, whether or not every member of the Amalekite tribe was murdered by the ancient Israelites. After all, "the universe doesn't care," and if the universe doesn't care, why should an atheist? Wilson claims that he can understand a nonbeliever who accepts nihilism, but he cannot understand one like Hitchens, who is unceasing in his moral condemnation of that which he regards as unjust. How, Wilson asks, can he defend his strong moral convictions?

Hitchens attempts to meet this challenge by appealing to the "instinct of solidarity" that human beings naturally feel toward one another. He seems to think that this instinct provides an objective basis for his principles. Unfortunately, that leaves him open to the objection that there are other instincts which are incompatible with this one, such as our instinct for waging war. Here is how Wilson puts it in the book:

> What I want to know (*still*) is what warrant you have for calling some [of these instinctive] behaviors "good" and others "wicked." If both are innate, what distinguishes them? What could be wrong with just flipping a coin?[122]

Of course, similar complaints can be raised against the theist side. Wilson thinks that by appealing to God, the question is settled, and seems unable to conceive how that might not be the case. Hitchens answers:

> I in turn ask you by what right you assume that a celestial autocracy is a guarantee of morals, let alone by what right you choose your own (Christian) version of it as the only correct one. All deities have been hailed by their subjects as the fount of good behavior, just as they have been used as the excuse for inexcusable behavior.[123]

The discussion ends without ever being resolved. As Hitchens himself admits, the two of them are "reasonably equally matched."[124]

A subjectivist, however, has no difficulty at all in answering Wilson. The universe may not care whether the Amalekites were utterly destroyed, but that doesn't stop any one of us from caring. And what *justifies* our feeling this way? That's the wrong sort of question. There doesn't have to *be* a justification. We care, and that's all; that's enough. Now, it is true that most people, given that they don't understand subjectivism, are not going to be satisfied with such an answer, especially if stated so succinctly. Wilson, I'm sure, would hardly be impressed. And so more needs to be said in order to provide one's opponent with the proper level of understanding. But once that's done, the reply to the theist is very simple indeed.

6

GOD AND THE UNIVERSE

> I do think the notion of the world having an explanation is a mistake... the universe is just there, and that's all.
>
> — Bertrand Russell

Over the last four chapters, we have seen reasons to rule out the existence of God whether he is understood as the Christian deity or more broadly as the omnipotent, omniscient, perfectly good being that most theists believe in. But this does not mean, of course, that no God whatsoever exists. There are many other possibilities. One could agree with the central conclusions presented in these chapters and still maintain that there is a supernatural being who – whatever his other characteristics – is responsible for the existence of everything else. For the remainder of the book, we will be primarily concerned with this more basic idea. The arguments we will cover are sufficiently general to apply to the core concept that unites all monotheists.

That there is a God in at least this minimal sense is something a great many people appear to find intuitively obvious. Whereas the specific doctrines of Christianity and of other religions may give rise to serious doubt – after all, even the most sincere believer occasionally wonders how the Christian God could allow millions to die of starvation – the simple conviction that a higher power exists is far more secure. That the universe is here at all, and moreover that it appears to have been put together with certain ends in mind, are for many people clear indicators of the reality of God. That is why some say that atheism requires more faith than theism. This does not mean that such philosophical considerations are the real reasons most people believe; the underlying cause is usually far more emotional than that, and is tied to religion. But the philosophical arguments do provide theists with a way of defending their position, at least up to a point.

Whether or not they provide good, *convincing* reasons is the topic to which we now turn.

GOD AS THE ULTIMATE CAUSE

We'll begin with the cosmological argument, which postulates that God is necessary as the explanation for why there is a universe at all. If a religious person is challenged on her belief in God, it is a pretty good bet that she will appeal to this kind of idea, perhaps by simply asking the question, "if there is no God, then where did everything come from?" There are a handful of "proofs" along these lines, the best-known being Aquinas's first-cause argument. This celebrated argument states that the chain of causes and effects cannot extend into the infinite past, and that therefore there had to be a first, uncaused cause – which of course is God. In recent years, a medieval

Islamic version of this same basic idea, known as the *Kalam cosmological argument*, was popularized by a philosopher already mentioned several times in these pages, William Lane Craig. It may be stated as follows:

> Whatever begins to exist has a cause of its existence. The universe began to exist. Therefore, the universe has a cause of its existence, and that is God.

We will concentrate on this version of the cosmological argument because it is easier to understand, has been defended at length by Craig, and appears to be the most popular one nowadays. Much of what will be said, however, applies every bit as much to Aquinas's version and to others in the same vein.

A few objections to the Kalam argument might immediately come to mind, perhaps the most obvious concerning the final claim: that the cause in question is God. Even if nothing else is wrong with the reasoning and it demonstrates that there was indeed a cause of everything else, how can we conclude that this cause is God? The fact that such a question doesn't even occur to most people shows that they are all-too-ready to accept a conclusion they find pleasing, whether or not they have actual grounds for doing so. A second problem involves the claim that whatever begins to exist has a cause. Though such a statement may at first appear to be nothing more than simple common sense, it needs support, as we shall see. In addition, it isn't clear that the universe must have had a beginning. Proponents of the argument claim that an infinite past is impossible, but of course that claim needs support as well. And finally, even if an infinite past is problematic, it isn't at all obvious that the introduction of

God removes the problem. On the face of it, it doesn't, for in that case it seems either that God has always existed – which reintroduces the problem of an infinite past – or else that he too began to exist, and thus also requires a cause. As it stands, then, this argument is at best incomplete. Much more needs to be said. Let's look at each of the four above issues, starting with whether or not the past must be finite.

(1) Craig uses two methods to show that the universe must have had a beginning in time. One consists of philosophical arguments aimed at demonstrating that an infinite past is somehow incoherent, and therefore impossible. The other is an appeal to science. To begin with, the philosophical arguments:

Craig starts out with the claim that it is impossible to get an actual infinite by means of successive addition. For instance, although one can in principle count forever, no matter how long one does so, one will never reach infinity. The infinite always remains a mere potential; it never becomes actual. But, Craig says, the "temporal series of events is a collection formed by successive addition."[125] Each event follows the previous one, and thus is "added" to it. It follows that the temporal series cannot be an actual infinite. Therefore, the universe must have had a beginning. In other words, it's as if someone has been counting each event in the history of the universe. If there was no beginning, then they have already been counting for an infinite time, and thus have already counted an infinite number of events. But if so, then they have reached infinity, which is impossible; infinity cannot be arrived at this way. Hence, the past cannot be infinite.

That one can never reach infinity by successive addition suggests a second argument: that there cannot be actual infinities at all, only potential ones. The infinite, according to this view, cannot exist in reality; it is only an idea in the minds of mathematicians. Craig backs up this second claim in a variety of ways meant to show that actual infinities would lead to absurdities. For example, he points out that if there were a library with an infinite number of books, sequentially numbered (1, 2, 3, etc.), then every single natural number would already be taken up. But then one could not add a new book to this collection, he says, for there would be *no number left* to assign to it. And that is absurd, since in reality "it obviously is possible to add to... a collection of books."[126]

But Craig is simply wrong. To begin with, his first argument is flawed because the two situations that he compares are not equivalent. A series that begins at some point, such as that of the natural numbers (1, 2, 3, ...), never reaches infinity. But the series of past events, if it is infinite, did *not* begin at some point prior to arriving at infinity; it never began, and thus *always has been* infinite. One may object to this for other reasons, but there is no "arriving at infinity" problem here, as Craig maintains. There never was a point, in other words, at which the number of events crossed the line between the finite and the infinite. Hence, his conclusion does not follow.

That the series has always been infinite, however, may be denied on the basis of the second argument, which states that there are no actual infinities – and that it is therefore impossible in principle for there to be an infinite collection of anything. To return to the library example, if each book in the collection already has a number, how can a new book be assigned its own number? As it turns out, though, there is a way to do so: all one has to do is renumber the collection. For instance, if we call the new book 1, then the book previously numbered 1 becomes book 2, the previous book 2 becomes book 3, and so on down the line. In this way, a number is once again available for every single volume in the collection. (The poor librarian would of course be kept busy for all of eternity, but that's not our problem.) This solution works because of an interesting property that infinite collections have, namely, that in their case, a part can be as large as the whole. In a *finite* collection, a part is of course always smaller. But in an infinite collection, that isn't necessarily so. The original infinite collection of books has the same size as the new collection to which one more book has been added. Infinity plus one isn't larger than infinity; infinity plus one is infinity.* (If you doubt that in an infinite collection a part can be as great as the whole, think of the even numbers, 2, 4, 6, and so on. It may seem that there are only half as many such numbers as there are natural numbers, since all the odd ones are missing. But now think of how one would go about counting the even numbers: "2" is the first, "4" is the second, and so on. It is obvious that each even number would in that case be paired with one natural number – namely, with the one that is its half. And that means that for each even number there is exactly one natural number, and vice versa. Thus, there are, surprisingly, as many even numbers as there are natural numbers.)

Now, Craig is aware of this solution, but objects that it again mistakes the potential with the actual. The solution, he says, works only if the number of books is *potentially* infinite, in which case one can continue adding new numbers to the total. With such a collection, the librarian can keep adding books and assigning them still unused

---

* There are different degrees of infinity, so that some infinites are larger than others, but that is a different matter.

numbers. But if she already had an infinite collection and were given one more book, she would find that no number is available to assign to it, he says. Craig's complaint here may also be understood this way. Forget for the moment the new book, and consider only the books that have been reassigned numbers, which are books 2 through infinity in the "new" collection. Since these books had originally been assigned numbers 1 through infinity, there must be one book left over, without a number. Or, to put it another way, the numbers 1 through infinity are one more than the numbers 2 through infinity. But that's simply not true, and it is very easy to demonstrate that it's not. Suppose that the librarian, when numbering the *original* infinite collection, before the new book arrived on the scene, had begun with 2 instead of 1. Would she have somehow run out of numbers? Of course not! There would still have been a number available for each book even if she had started with 2 – or for that matter, if she had started with a trillion trillion. Craig maintains that it is ridiculous to suppose that the initial collection is the same size as that collection plus one, but he's wrong. I admit that infinity is counterintuitive, but to complain that it is impossible for a part to be the same size as a whole, as Craig does, is to apply the rules for a *finite* set to an infinite set, and that's simply a mistake.

At any rate, the claim that no actual infinities exist is demonstrably false. There are literally an infinite number of examples of infinity around you right now. Consider that every time you walk from one place to another – in fact, every time you take even one step – you go through an infinite number of subdivisions of the distance: you first go through the halfway point, then the 3/4 of the way point, the 7/8 point, and so on *ad infinitum*. Nor is it the case that these are only *potential* subdivisions

(subdivisions we could in principle keep making forever without ever finishing our task), as is often claimed. The subdivisions are actual, not merely potential, because *they are already there*. They do not first have to be demarcated by us in order to exist; they exist in their own right. The halfway point between any two locations is there, whether anyone takes notice of it or not – and likewise for all the other points along the path. In demarcating the subdivisions we do not create them, we merely set them apart from one another.

There are many other cases of actual infinity – again, an infinite number of them. Consider the number pi, which has a non-repeating decimal expansion that begins 3.14159 and goes on forever. Now, there is a matter of fact regarding every number in this expansion. For instance, when it was first established that the fifth place after the decimal is a nine, that was a discovery; it was already true beforehand – and similarly for any place in pi's decimal expansion. But in that case, the facts about pi's decimal expansion represent an actual infinity. Now, we can think of these facts as numbered, like Craig's books, and ask whether or not we can add another fact to this collection. (Any fact will do for our purposes, e.g., "the Pope is Catholic.") If Craig's argument were valid, there would be a problem here: since all the numbers have already been taken up, there would be no room for any additional facts – which is another way of saying that there could not *be* any additional facts. But just as sure as the Pope is Catholic, there are. Actually, there are an infinite number of additional facts, including the fact that Craig's argument is wrong.

Craig has not succeeded in showing that the past must be finite using logic alone. However, as previously mentioned, he also uses a scientific method to support the notion of a finite past: he appeals to cosmology. Our universe, scientists believe, began with a cataclysmic event, the big bang, approximately 13.8 billion years ago. Hence, even without resorting to any supposed incoherence associated with infinity, one might maintain that in fact things have not been around forever.

Now, this argument is certainly better than the previous ones, for it at least provides us with some reason to suppose that the universe began. Nevertheless, it is flawed as well. The big bang is not necessarily the absolute beginning. The only thing that is fairly clear is that it was the starting point of the *current state* of the universe. It's not at all certain that nothing preceded it. Many scientists nowadays lean towards the hypothesis that there was a pre-existing state, though what exactly that was is open to debate. A number of theories have been proposed, all of them (even if informed by what are currently the best-established theories) rather speculative. No one really knows. But to argue, as Craig does, that the big bang is the absolute beginning is to go well beyond the available evidence.

(2) Suppose, however, that the universe hasn't been around forever – which, after all, may very well be the case. Does it follow that it must have had a cause? At this point, most people would probably concede the point to Craig. To hold that, for instance, the big bang might have occurred for no reason at all may seem ridiculous. How could the universe – or anything else – have come into being unless caused to do so? It doesn't even sound possible for a single pebble to suddenly materialize out of nothing. How much more improbable, then, for such a thing to be the case with respect to the entire universe! And yet, no matter how obvious this point might seem, it is in fact problematic.

In the first place, if the universe began because an infinite past is impossible, as Craig and some others maintain, then that means that *time* began as well. And in that case, there was nothing that happened before – since there *was* no before – and so there could not have been a cause that preceded the universe. Even worse, the above makes a comparison between the universe having an uncaused beginning and something like a pebble "popping" into existence. The two are not analogous, however. If the universe had a beginning in time, then it did not suddenly appear out of nothing – for the very simple reason that *there was no prior time during which there was nothing*. Those who make such a comparison present us with a picture of the situation that is in fact misleading: they suppose that there is nothingness, followed by a universe suddenly materializing. As Craig himself put it, "if originally there were absolutely nothing – no God, no space, no time – then how could the universe possibly come to exist?"[127] That is not what a beginning to time itself means. There wasn't "originally" nothing – including no time – since of course there wasn't a *time* when there was no time! If things began at some point (say, at the big bang), then the universe has in a sense "always" existed; it has existed, that is, at *every moment* of time. In this scenario, then, the universe simply exists – just as it does in the scenario in which there is no beginning – with the only difference that it has not existed forever because *time itself* is finite. What the universe does not do is arise from nothing: there is never a time when there is nothing for it to arise out of.

There are many unanswered questions about this scenario, of course, but there isn't a problem regarding how the universe came into being in this case. It didn't *come into being* at all. It simply exists.

(3) For the sake of argument, though, let's move on to the next stage and assume that the universe both began to exist and had an external cause. The next question we need to address is why this cause is supposed to be God. Why think that a conscious being was involved? On this issue, Craig appeals to a distinction between personal causation and physical causation. Personal causation is what is involved when a free-willed agent decides to do something, whereas physical causation is what we see in the inanimate world – for instance, when gravity causes a rock to tumble down a hill. The latter type of causation, Craig maintains, produces its effects automatically: with necessary and sufficient conditions in place, the result is inevitable. The former, though, since it is dependent on free will, does not. Thus, if the cause of the big bang were physical in nature and had existed from all eternity, then the effect would also have existed from all eternity – just as if the temperature had been below freezing all along, then any water would already have been frozen for that entire time. A mind, on the other hand, could have existed from eternity and yet choose to bring about the universe at some specific moment. Unlike a physical cause, a mind can freely choose "to create an effect in time without any prior determining conditions. For example, a man sitting from eternity could freely will to stand up."[128] God, then, might have existed forever and then, out of the blue, decide to create the universe. Thus, the cause of the universe must be a personal being.

The reader may at this point be wondering how Craig can talk about God's eternity – or for that matter how he can entertain the possibility of a physical cause existing from eternity – when he denies an infinite past, but let's leave that aside for now; we will return to this issue in the next section. Even ignoring this problem, however, at least two additional things must be true in order for the current argument to work. It must be the case that there is such a thing as free will, and it must be the case that such free agent causation is the only alternative to deterministic physical causation. In the next chapter I will argue that the first claim is not true: there is no such thing as free will because the concept of free will is incoherent and thus cannot apply to anything. But the second claim is not necessarily true either. Most physicists believe that there is genuine randomness in nature. If so, then it is possible for a set of conditions to exist without an effect resulting immediately. An atom of uranium, for example, is such that it might break down in the next millisecond or – under apparently the exact same conditions – not do so for a million years. If it makes sense for a free agent to exist "from eternity" prior to making a decision, then it appears much the same could be said regarding physical conditions that operate with a certain degree of indeterminacy. At the very least, it seems to make no more sense to claim such a thing about free actions than about random events. This part of the argument therefore also fails.

(4) The last question we need to address concerns God's own eternity. If the universe began to exist because the past is finite, then God cannot have been around forever either. But then the problem of a causeless beginning (if one insists that it is indeed a problem) merely gets transferred to God. And if instead God *has* been around forever, then of course the past must be infinite – and in that case why couldn't it be the universe that has always existed instead?

The standard theological solution at this point is to maintain that God is timeless. That way he neither came into being nor has existed for an infinite amount of time. And yet how a timeless being can create a universe – or do anything for that matter – is unclear. A timeless being pretty much just sits around doing nothing; that's what it means to be timeless. Craig attempts to avoid this problem by making God timeless "prior" to creation, and temporal afterwards. But if that makes sense with respect to God, why couldn't it make sense with respect to something else – with some as yet unknown stuff out of which the universe was created at the big bang?

The introduction of God to remove concerns about infinity also raises a serious difficulty for anyone who believes in the traditional Judeo-Christian-Islamic God (which of course includes Craig himself), for this God is himself infinite, and has infinite powers. If no actual infinities can exist, how can there be a God? In reply, Craig insists that in God's case the situation is different: "the infinity of God's being," he says, "has nothing to do with an actually infinite collection of definite and distinct finite members."[129] To put it another way, God isn't made up of parts, so his limitlessness isn't a problem. But the distinction Craig is going for here cannot reasonably be maintained. God presumably knows the entire decimal expansion of pi, for example, and if that is the case, then that is an actual infinity, comprised of "definite and distinct members," existing in God's mind. It follows that if Craig's arguments against infinity were correct, he would have proved that traditional theism is false. (His arguments unfortunately fail, however, and he therefore cannot be given such an honor.)

As we have seen, the Kalam cosmological argument is beset with far too many problems to be considered as evidence – even of an extremely weak kind – for the existence of God. Furthermore, the same thing can be said regarding Aquinas's first-cause argument and similar ones that attempt to prove that a deity is needed as the cause

177

of the universe. None of the cosmological arguments work. Whatever the true origin of things, there is no reason whatsoever to claim that some conscious being had to be involved in the process.

WHY IS THERE SOMETHING RATHER THAN NOTHING?

The initial plausibility of the cosmological argument comes from the feeling many have that there has to be an ultimate reason for the fact of existence itself. That there is something rather than nothing, it seems, calls out for explanation – and the conventional view is that the atheist cannot provide one. Now, I happen to think that last part is right: the atheist cannot provide an explanation for the fact of existence itself. But then neither can anyone else. It's important to realize that the idea of God alone does not answer the question "where did everything come from?" A creator might provide an explanation for the existence of everything *other than himself*, but in that case we would still have to ask about his own existence. With respect to the ultimate question, then, the theist and the atheist are in the same boat. Neither can account for the fact that there is something rather than nothing. The only thing the theist does that's different is introduce one more entity into the mix – and a rather implausible one at that. If the fact of existence requires explanation, the atheist needs to explain the physical universe; the theist, on the other hand, needs to explain the physical universe *and* God. That doesn't seem to be much of an improvement.

In my opinion, in any case, no explanation is necessary for existence as such. I don't at all share Richard Swinburne's intuition when he says:

> It is extraordinary that there should exist anything at all. Surely the most natural state of affairs is simply nothing: no universe, no God, nothing. But there is something. And so many things. Maybe chance could have thrown up the odd electron. BUT *so* many particles![130]

Why is nothingness "the most natural state of affairs"? Why, after all, should there be nothing rather than something? That seems at least as reasonable a thing to ask as the more common "why is there something rather than nothing?" On one way of looking at it, all metaphysically possible states of affairs, including nothingness, can be thought of as on an equal footing, so the fact that this universe exists is no more mysterious than any other universe existing, or than there being no universe at all. And for some, it goes further than that: it is the idea of true nothingness that seems profoundly strange. Could there really be nothing at all – perhaps not even space or time? Maybe, but it's difficult to even imagine such a state.

In spite of this, it is natural to suppose that "nothing" requires no explanation, since it is the simplest possible state. Many people think that "something" does require one, however. And yet, unless there is some entity that is self-explanatory (whatever that might mean), not *everything* will have an explanation – and therefore existence itself won't. Swinburne admits as much. He accepts the fact that we must begin somewhere, with something whose existence is a "brute fact," and proceed to account for everything else on the basis of that. But of course he thinks that this something is God, a "simple being" whose existence, he thinks, is much less mysterious than the existence of other things. And yet God is an entity for which we have no evidence, a being with powers that are unlike anything we have ever encountered, and one whose mode of existence would be unlike that of anything else that we are aware of. We cannot postulate God without making some pretty large assumptions. On the other hand, we do know that the physical universe exists. If something must be accepted as a brute fact, then, it seems that the physical universe is a much better candidate. Perhaps, then, as Bertrand Russell said, it really "is just there, and that's all."[131]

FROM WATCHMAKERS TO IRREDUCIBLE COMPLEXITY

The other popular reason offered for the existence of God is the design argument. Though its basic idea is an old one, going back to antiquity, the argument found its classical expression in *Natural Theology*, an 1802 volume by British philosopher and naturalist William Paley. In this work – which influenced the young Charles Darwin, among others – Paley asks us to imagine finding a watch in the wilderness. Even if we had never seen such an object, he says, we would right away conclude that it was made by some intelligent being. A watch is too complex, and shows too many signs of intentional purpose, for it to be the sort of thing that could have formed by accident. Where there's a watch, then, there must be a watchmaker. But now compare this with the apparent design we find in nature, and in particular in organisms. The human eye, for example, is more complex than a watch, and it too serves a purpose. If a watch requires a maker, then, the eye must require one as well. And not just the eye, of course. A particularly amusing contemporary version of this argument, popularized by minister and evangelist Ray

Comfort, asks us to consider the lowly banana. It too shows evidence of being intentionally made. For instance, it has outward indicators of its inner contents: when green it is too early to consume, when yellow it is just right, and when black it is too late. It has a sort of "tab" at one end and ridges along its sides, all to make it easy to peel. It has a non-slip surface that fits perfectly into the human hand. And, as Comfort explains, it is even pointed at the top for "ease of entry" (his words) into the human mouth. No wonder he calls the banana "the atheist's nightmare"[132] (although by this logic, it would seem that the coconut must have been designed by Satan himself).

Comfort's particular version of the argument suffers from the inconvenient fact that the bananas we are familiar with today were bred by farmers over the last few thousand years. Breeding works on the same principle as other cases of evolution except that human beings choose the individual plants or animals that get to pass along their genes, and thus to a great extent select which characteristics a given organism will have. It is for this reason that the bananas one finds at the supermarket are much more user-friendly than the original wild variety. Comfort's idea, then, can easily be dismissed. The design argument, however, does not have to be limited to domesticated organisms, and Paley's more basic version therefore still convinces many people – even if it, too, has lost much of its force as a result of the theory of evolution.

Darwin produced an alternative account of the development of organisms, and by doing so superseded Paley. It is possible to accept evolution and still be a theist, of course, but the important point is that evolution does away with any *need* to posit a maker for biological systems. Natural selection explains how complexity can arise gradually, over eons of time, without plan or purpose. The basic idea is not at all complicated: in any given population, there are differences among the individual members. For instance, in a group of humans, some are better runners than others, some have sharper eyesight than others, and so on. Now, certain of these characteristics will confer an advantage to the individuals that possess them (depending on what challenges their particular environment presents them with). Those individuals that have an advantage have slightly better prospects of passing on their genes to the next generation, and thus of having their advantageous characteristics inherited. As a result, the population as a whole changes over time. (Natural selection, it should be said, is not the only cause of change in populations, but it is the most important one.) To consider a simple example, take the color of the polar bear. Because of a genetic mutation, white or light-colored specimens appear occasionally in other bear species – including in the brown bear, from which the polar bear is descended. Now, in the brown bear's environment, light-colored fur does not offer any benefits – quite the opposite, in fact; in the arctic, however, it certainly does. A dark bear would much more easily be seen by its potential prey than a light one. Thus, through the pressures of natural selection, populations of bears that moved north gradually turned white.

The evolution of something as complex as the eye may not be as obvious, but nevertheless involves the same basic principle. One can trace the development of vision back to almost the simplest life-forms. Light-sensitive proteins are found even in many single-celled creatures, and it is not uncommon for primitive multicellular animals to have "eyespots" composed of photoreceptor cells. On somewhat more advanced organisms, such cells are found on slightly concave surfaces – something that helps the animal detect the direction of the light source. The more concave the better, and so, much further along this evolutionary process, one finds creatures with primitive eyes consisting of a cavity with only a "pinhole" opening left to let the light in – much as in the earliest cameras. A transparent, jelly-like covering protecting the photo-receptor cells offers yet another advantage, and – as Dawkins points out – can very easily begin to take on a curved shape and work as a primitive lens (in fact, such shapes are commonly found in nature even in objects that do not function as lenses, like water droplets or the bodies of jellyfish). From there, the development of even the most advanced eyes is not so difficult to visualize. Eyes have actually arisen independently numerous times throughout the animal kingdom, and the evolution from a flat eyespot with a transparent protective surface to a simple eye like that of a fish has been conservatively estimated, by means of computer models, to be capable of occurring within half a million years – a length of time that, geologically speaking, is extremely short.[133]

In spite of overwhelming evidence in its favor – from DNA, the fossil record, comparative anatomy, biogeography, vestigial structures, and so on – not everyone accepts Darwin's theory. Of course the great majority of naysayers are simply people who don't understand how evolution works or what the evidence for it is. And in many cases, even when the principle is explained to them, people find it hard to believe. The immense time scales involved, which are necessary for the process to work, are difficult to imagine. As Dawkins notes, the error of a young earth creationist, who supposes our planet to be between six and ten thousand years old, is on the same order as that of someone who imagines the distance from New York to Los Angeles to be less than 30 feet. But there are more-or-less sophisticated objections to evolution as well. Let's briefly look at the most serious of these, the argument from irreducible complexity made by biochemist Michael Behe. This is a well-known criticism of Darwin that is in fact nothing less than a new form of the design argument.

Behe accepts evolution up to a point – that is, he believes in common descent, as well as in an old earth – but maintains that there are certain structures in cells, such as the bacterial flagellum, that are just too complex to have evolved. The structures in question have a number of essential parts working in unison, so that if even one were missing, the whole would no longer be able to function. It is this complexity that Behe calls "irreducible": all parts need to be present before the mechanism can perform its job. But if that is the case, then how could the entire structure have appeared in the first place? It is statistically impossible for all of the parts of any such mechanism, organized in just the right way, to have accidentally appeared simultaneously, as a result of random mutations. And if that is the case, then the only alternative that makes sense to Behe is that of an intelligent designer.

But even though the argument from irreducible complexity has received a lot of attention in recent years, it is nothing more than a rehashing of an old objection to evolution to which the answer is already known. Some of the earliest critics of Darwin insisted that his theory made no sense because, while it was impossible for something as complex as a wing or an eye to appear all at once, a *partial* wing or partial eye would be useless. For instance, an early bird species with "half a wing" would not be able to fly with it, and thus such a structure would not benefit the bird in any way. How then did the full wing ever get a chance to develop? We've already seen the answer to this sort of objection with respect to the eye: a "half eye" is in fact useful. It may not provide its owner with a sharp image of the outside world, but it does provide it with *some* information, and that's better than nothing. Similarly in the case of the wing: the proto-wings in the dinosaurian ancestors of birds, for instance, may have been used for balance. And gliding, even if it isn't quite as desirable as flying, is certainly preferable to falling. Partial wings, then, are perfectly sensible and understandable. Furthermore, evolution works on whatever structures already exist, and this means that the components in complex structures may have originally served a different function. Feathers, without which birds could not fly, were probably first useful for warmth, and perhaps in courtship displays, and only later adapted for the purpose of flying. The answer to Behe's challenge, then, is simple. The parts of the bacterium flagellum, or of any other complex structure that one cares to consider, were perfectly capable of evolving independently and of having been originally retained for different reasons. Scientists have proposed detailed explanations along these lines for Behe's supposed cases of irreducible complexity – and given all of the evidence in favor of evolution, the onus of proof is on Behe and his supporters to demonstrate that nothing like what these scientists have suggested is even possible.

Evolution, as much as creationists hate to hear it, is a fact. But that does not mean that it has completely done away with the design argument. The truth is that it has not done so, for one very simple reason: the argument is not limited to the biological world. In Paley's day many also saw the clock-like operation of the heavens and other such things as evidence of a creator. A modern version of the same general idea is the fine-tuning argument, which we will consider in the final section of this chapter. A thorough criticism of the design argument therefore must include non-Darwinian objections as well, and so before anything else we shall consider some of these.

HUME'S OBJECTIONS

It is an ironic but well-known fact that even before Paley's book was written, the design argument had already suffered devastating criticism at the hands of the 18th-century Scottish philosopher David Hume, in his posthumously published *Dialogues Concerning Natural Religion*. Many of Hume's objections are applicable to more modern versions of the argument as well. Here, I will not attempt to cover every point made by the great Scot, nor consider every detail in each; a few of the main ones are sufficient for our purposes. As we will see, a couple of them in particular are decisive.

To begin with, Hume questions the strength of the analogies made in arguments like Paley's. There is more than one problem here. Consider the fact that the watches in our world were produced, not by one being – and certainly not by an immaterial, immortal, all-powerful and perfectly good being – but by many physical, mortal, imperfect ones. Watchmakers throughout history have learned from others in their profession, and have improved on earlier ideas. A more sensible conclusion to draw from the analogy, then, is not that a single non-physical God exists, but that many imperfect and physical gods do – and also that perhaps they learn from each other's mistakes. But such a polytheistic result is not at all what proponents of the design argument have in mind. In fact, they might find the idea rather shocking.

Just as there is a disanalogy between watchmakers and God, there is one between watches and the natural world. According to Hume, nature is in many respects less like a human artifact than it is like an organism. For, as with the latter, a "continual circulation of matter in it produces no disorder," and "a continual waste in every part is incessantly repaired."[134] But if it is more like an organism than like a machine, then its cause too might be more akin to the cause of an animal or plant. And so "its origin ought rather to be ascribed to generation or vegetation than to reason or design."[135] Add to this the fact that intelligence or consciousness, as far as has been observed, requires an organism before it can even exist, and the point becomes even more forceful. Minds arise as a result of preexisting biology, not the other way around. It would be more logical, therefore, to suppose that the ultimate cause lies in some physical biological system rather than in a mind.

At this point, Hume has subtly moved from mere weaknesses in the analogy to a more fundamental objection: why must the ultimate reason for everything be mental rather than physical? In a particularly colorful passage, he tells us that according to some Hindus, "the world arose from an infinite spider, who spun this whole complicated mass from his bowels." Of course, such an arachnid-based cosmogony seems ridiculous to us, but that's not the point. The important thing is that there is no good reason why, as Hume put it, "an orderly system may not be spun from the belly as well as from the brain."[136] It is true that an ultimate explanation that is physical appears inadequate to most of us. If one is suggested, we immediately want to know what caused it. With regards to the current example, for instance, we want to know just where the giant spider came from. If the ultimate explanation is claimed to be mental, on the other hand, most of us are satisfied. It doesn't even occur to most people that there might be a problem concerning God's origins; his existence is accepted as a given. However, is there any basis for such a distinction between the mental and the physical, or is this perhaps mere bias on our part?

It seems to me that our tendency to more readily accept uncreated spiritual entities is related to certain erroneous intuitions most of us have about the mind. I will have more to say about that in the next chapter, where we will examine the common-sense view on this and its connection with theism. The current objection, however, naturally leads to another which is, in my opinion, the strongest of all of Hume's criticisms. It is also a very simple one: if the universe, as a result of its organization and complexity, requires an explanation, Hume asks, then why doesn't God need one as well? To posit God as the explanation for the complexity of the universe gets us nowhere. It merely takes things one step further, at which point the same problem arises all over again. In this respect, the argument is like the ancient Hindu view that the earth rests on top of a giant turtle. This immediately raises the question, what does the giant turtle rest on? Perhaps it is turtles "all the way down," as some say. Similarly, God may have been designed by some super-God, and this super-God in turn by a super-super-God, and so on, *ad infinitum*. But once again, such an idea will appear absurd – and even blasphemous – to most theists. They want to go no further than the first deity.

This "who designed God" objection is well-known, and there are a couple of common replies available. The first is this. Whenever someone explains one thing by means of another, it is, as a general rule, a mistake to insist that they must also be able to explain the second thing. The existence of watches is accounted for by the existence of human beings, and in order for this to be reasonable one does not also have to be able to explain *our* existence. Even if one does not know where humanity came from, one can still appeal to it as the reason for why there are watches. Similarly, it is claimed, the universe can be said to be the work of God, and it is not thereby necessary to explain God. Reasons can only go so far. If one were to insist on an explanation for everything, then one would indeed end up with an infinite regress, as in the above series of gods and super-gods. But one must of course begin somewhere, and according to this way of thinking, it is perfectly proper to begin with God. He is the starting point, so to speak.

The problem with this reply, though, is that it misses the main point of the objection. Hume's complaint is not based on the idea that everything must have an explanation. Rather, it is based on the idea – on which the design argument depends – that *whatever is complex and organized* requires an explanation. The universe, Paley in effect says, must have a cause because of the way it is put together. Anything that exhibits such an arrangement of its parts cannot simply have come about of its own account. It must therefore have been the result of planning. But now the problem with this move should be apparent. God, too, is presumably complex – in fact, far more complex than the universe. Thus, if the universe requires a designer, then God must require one as well. And in that case, we may in fact be stuck with an infinite regress.

The second reply to this "who designed God" objection picks up where the first one leaves off. Many theists, as it turns out, deny that God is complex. In fact, they claim that he is perfectly simple. This, as was briefly mentioned above, is Swinburne's view. But how can a being as amazing as the creator of the universe fail to be complex?

The principal argument for the simplicity of God is that, being a non-physical entity, God has no parts. This is an idea that goes at least as far back as Plato, who regarded the soul as lacking complexity for this very reason. (In fact, this was one way Plato argued for the immortality of the soul: if it has no parts, then it cannot disintegrate – the way the body does – after death.) But even if a soul or mind is simple in that it has no parts, that does not mean it is simple in every respect. Even proponents of this "simple soul hypothesis" sometimes admit that a mind can be complex in other ways. Theist philosophers Stewart Goetz and Charles Taliaferro, for instance, write that a "soul that is by hypothesis substantively simple (without structure or complexity at the level of thinghood) can be structured or complex at the level of properties. Stated differently, a lack of substantive parts is compatible with a multiplicity of properties."[137] Or in other words, a mind can be simple in that it has no parts and yet be complex in that it has many abilities and holds a variety of information. But this is fatal to the design argument, for the complexity of the contents of God's mind is as much in need of explanation as the complexity of the physical world. There is no non-arbitrary reason for demanding such an explanation for the world and maintaining that it isn't needed for God's mental properties.

So far we have covered three main Humean objections to the design argument. The fourth and final one we will consider is something we might call the problem of imperfection, which can be seen from (as Hume puts it) "the inaccurate workmanship of all the springs and principles of the great machine of nature."[138] For, in spite of the fact that everything in the world around us seems to serve some purpose, nature is not so finely calibrated that it can always be counted upon – far from it. Plants and animals need rain, but all too often there is either not enough of it, or else there is too much – and similarly with everything else on this planet. The already discussed problem of evil is the most important and most obvious example of imperfection in nature, but there are flaws on a smaller scale which also count against belief in a cosmic architect. Imagine that we found a watch with obvious design flaws, one that did not keep very accurate time and every once in a while got stuck. We would conclude that the watchmaker was also less than perfect. But now consider the human eye. True, it may be a wonder of nature, but that doesn't mean it's flawless. For one thing, it has a blind spot: there is a small area where the optic nerve connects to the inside of each eye that has no photoreceptor cells. We normally do not notice this because we have two eyes (so that what lies in the blind spot of one eye is usually in the field of vision of the other), and also because – strangely enough – even when we look out of only one eye, our brain fills in that area with what it *expects* to be there (which means that sometimes we are actually tricked into experiencing something that isn't there). Now, this is clearly an imperfection. There appears to be no logical reason for the internal structure of the eye to be set up this way – and in fact, the eyes of the cephalopods, like the octopus and squid (which evolved independently of our own), do not have such a blind spot. The optic nerve in their case connects behind the retina, and thus does not block out any of their field of vision. And there are many other such cases of imperfections in nature. Consider the fact that our jaws are too small to accommodate our wisdom teeth, that women have a very difficult time in childbirth, and that our back muscles are rather weak, causing the all-too-common back problems that many of us experience. If all of this is the work of a designer, then that designer does not appear to have done the very best job possible.

One thing a theist could say is that the creator *is* less than perfect. As I've already pointed out, the design argument need not be an argument for the all-powerful, all-good being that most theists believe in; it can instead be an argument for the God of the deists – a God who perhaps isn't quite as concerned with us as the Christian one is said to be. But the difficulty is actually worse than that, and even deists might have a hard time justifying what we observe. Any being with the ability to create a person or an entire solar system should be able to see that our eye design is less than fully desirable. So why didn't he make our eyes like those of the octopus? And anyway, what is the point of making our eyes one way and those of other creatures a different way? Again, perhaps there are many imperfect gods, and the one in charge of our vision was a bit of an underachiever. But there is a far more reasonable alternative: the one Darwin proposed. The imperfections found in nature are further evidence for evolution. Natural selection works on what it has available to work with; it does not plan ahead. Random mutations occur, and the environment puts pressure on organisms so that certain of these mutations are favored over others. Under the circumstances, the design of the human eye was the best nature could do. A different set of events allowed for a superior design in the case of the cephalopods. And similarly with the other examples. The recent development of bipedalism in our species accounts for the weakness of our back muscles, while the pain that women experience in childbirth is due, not to God unfairly punishing all women for the actions of Eve (as scripture would have us believe), but rather to the increase in brain size that our species has undergone (which makes the baby's head rather large in comparison with the birth canal). Many other such quirks point toward natural selection and away from an intelligent designer. And as to the rain, sunshine, wind, and the rest not always harmonizing with our needs, that too can be explained by evolution. These things were not set up for the purpose of serving the needs of creatures; rather, creatures evolved to make the best use they could of them. Thus, the earth usually provides what we need, but not always: there is no guarantee that it will do so. And this is exactly what we should expect. Unlike God, nature does *not* work in mysterious ways. Indeed, what would have been surprising, given our relatively random origins, is if everything had turned out perfectly.

A FINE-TUNED UNIVERSE?

That organisms are complex and built for survival can be explained naturalistically. That the environment is suitable for these organisms, as we've just seen with respect to such things as rain and warmth, can also be explained without recourse to a designer. Why there is an earth at all – that is, why there is a planet with the right conditions to allow life to develop – is also no great mystery: in a universe as vast as ours, with so many stars and planets, chances are there will be at least some worlds that just happen to be capable of sustaining life. The proponents of the design argument still have one move available to them, however. They can ask why the *universe itself* has the right properties. After all, it did not have to be this way. If either the laws of nature or the initial conditions at the big bang had been different, the result could have been utterly lifeless. The universe might, for instance, have consisted of particles that never combined into atoms or molecules at all; or it might at least have failed to have any stars and planets; it might not have had carbon – a material without which life as we know it could not exist; and there are countless other possibilities. Instead, it has just the right set of properties to allow complex biological systems to evolve, develop, and even to reach the point where some of them ask why the universe is the way it is.

The fine-tuning argument proceeds from the supposition that it was extremely unlikely for things to have turned out this way. Life-prohibiting universes are far more probable, supporters of the view maintain, than life-permitting ones. According to some, to say that it was extremely unlikely is actually an understatement, for the improbabilities involved are nothing short of mind-boggling. Stephen Hawking (though not a proponent of the argument) has said that if one second after the big bang the expansion rate had been smaller by one part in a hundred quadrillion (10^{17}), the universe would long ago have collapsed back on itself.[139] Even more astounding, some claim that the ratio of the electromagnetic force to gravity cannot deviate by more than one part in 10^{40}, and that several other values on which our existence depends are even more finely tuned than that.[140] William Lane Craig (who *is* a proponent of the argument) claims there are "around 50 such quantities and constants."[141] Now, I've never seen Craig's list, or any other that specifies nearly that many quantities – and there is also the question whether all these quantities are independent of one another – but the exact number isn't too important. The fact remains that, if even a single factor such as the one mentioned by Hawking is correct, it appears almost impossible for what we ended up with to have been the result of mere chance. The conclusion seems to be that someone set the dials, so to speak, in order to ensure that life could arise. As astronomer Fred Hoyle observed, it looks as if someone "has monkeyed with the laws of physics."[142]

As an argument for God's existence, the notion of fine-tuning certainly sounds impressive. In fact, it is probably the claim on the theist side that people tend to find the most compelling. Many atheists find it a difficult one to answer. In the documentary movie *Collision*, for instance, Christopher Hitchens calls the fine-tuning argument "intriguing" and admits it's far from trivial. And plenty of other nonbelievers have struggled with it. As soon as one looks at it more closely, however, the argument's initial plausibility begins to unravel – and when all is said and done, as we will see, it ends up meaning absolutely nothing.

By far the most popular response to the argument is the so-called multiverse hypothesis, so we'll begin with that. The basic idea that underlies this hypothesis is simple: perhaps the universe we are directly aware of is not all there is; there might instead be untold billions – and maybe even an infinite number – of other "universes" out there. If so, and if the conditions in these other worlds vary more or less randomly, then it should be the case that, while most may very well be barren, at least some will have the right conditions for life – and we, of course, are going to find ourselves in one of these latter kinds of universe, for only where there are the right sort of conditions can there be creatures to wonder about those conditions. That our cosmos is capable of supporting our existence would in that case be no more mysterious than that, out of the countless planets in our universe, at least some like the earth are capable of doing so. We at least have a choice, then: either God or a multiplicity of universes. And the latter, being naturalistic and essentially an extension of the scientific worldview we already have, seems the preferable alternative.

This multiverse hypothesis, it should be noted, is not simply (as some religionists cynically suggest) an *ad hoc* move on the part of atheistic scientists to avoid at all costs the possibility of a creator. The notion that the observable cosmos might not be all there is has been around longer than the fine-tuning argument. There are in fact several different theories as to why and how reality might consist of multiple worlds. For example, there is the possibility that the big bang was not the origin in any absolute sense, but instead that we might live in an "oscillating universe," made up of a series of cycles. Each cycle begins with a big bang, which leads to a period of expansion, is then followed by a period of contraction, and eventually ends in a "big crunch," at which point the cycle begins anew. This allows for the possibility of an infinite number of incarnations of the cosmos (and also does away with the apparent problem of a beginning). There are, it must be said, some difficulties with this view, though. If the laws of nature get shuffled at the start of each cycle (as must be the case if this proposal is to serve as a reply to the fine-tuning argument), then one result, it seems, might be a stage with laws that cause the universe to continue expanding forever. But then the series of cycles would come to an end, perhaps before life ever got a chance to arise. And the fact that the universe's current expansion is accelerating − thus suggesting that the universe will not contract again − further weakens this theory. The oscillating universe hypothesis, then, isn't the best reply to the concept of fine tuning.

A preferable solution is the idea that there are many "island universes," each an expanding "bubble" in a much larger space. This view of things is actually predicted by inflation theory, a theory which postulates a rapid period of expansion early in the history of the universe and which has been confirmed by recent observations. Such a multiverse is really just an amplification of our physical universe, and is accepted by a majority of cosmologists working today.[143]

As might be expected, the multiverse hypothesis has met with considerable resistance from the proponents of fine tuning. In particular, they have criticized it for being a far less simple theory than theism. Whereas the latter postulates the existence of just one entity, God, the former asks us to accept the existence of untold millions of other universes. Thus, by the principle known as Ockham's Razor – which states that we should assume no more than is necessary for our explanatory purposes – theism is thought to be the better hypothesis. It's not as simple as that, however. The question is not literally how many entities one postulates; the question is how unlikely one's assumptions are. The multiverse hypothesis postulates the existence of additional realms that are more or less like the physical universe which we already know exists, and furthermore does so on the basis of known scientific laws. Theism, on the other hand, asks us to accept the existence of a completely different sort of entity, without scientific support of any kind. It is theism therefore that appears to make the greater assumption, the one that takes us further beyond what we have evidence for. To better appreciate this point, consider once again Hume's giant spider hypothesis, mentioned in the previous section. It too postulates only one entity – and yet it obviously asks us to assume far more than the multiverse theory. After all, what are the chances a giant spider, of all things, might be responsible for the existence of stars, planets, and galaxies?

Though the multiverse idea provides us with an alternative explanation of things, there are other replies to the notion of fine tuning which make for even stronger objections to it. To begin with, the numerical values involved tend to be greatly exaggerated by proponents of the argument. Take the rate of the expansion of the universe mentioned by Hawking, which has been quoted to great effect by Craig,[144] Dinesh D'Souza,[145] and others. Hawking himself points out, later in the same work, how inflation theory accounts for the apparent fine-tuning in this case, "without having to assume that the initial rate of expansion of the universe was very carefully chosen."[146] This fact is conveniently ignored by Craig and D'Souza. There is also a great deal of disagreement with respect to at least some of the other values. The ratio of the force of gravity to electromagnetism is a case in point. Above, I mentioned that according to some, this ratio must be fine-tuned to one part in 10^{40} – an extraordinarily precise value, involving a number so large that it cannot truly be grasped. And yet astrophysicist Bernard Haisch, a theist and supporter of the fine-tuning argument, merely states that "if the gravitational force were 10 times stronger than it is, relative to the electric force, stars would be smaller and have shorter life times…" and that "if gravity were much weaker, far fewer stars would form, hence far fewer planets on which life can arise."[147] Not only is this quite a difference in estimates, the new values hardly qualify as fine tuning. This example shows that one cannot always trust the various claims that are made in favor of the argument.

Many critics have also disputed the claim that life could not exist in most types of possible universe. Perhaps life as we know it could not exist, but that doesn't mean there couldn't be some very different alien life forms. In reply, proponents of fine tuning point out that the great majority of possible universes would lack the conditions for any sort of life whatsoever: a universe consisting of nothing more complex than fundamental particles, or one that quickly collapsed back on itself after the big bang, or even one that contained no elements heavier than helium, could not support biology of any kind, no matter how different it might be. So it may seem that the proponents of the argument come out ahead on this one point at least. But even here there are problems for their side. First, it is far from clear that such extreme life-prohibiting conditions would be found in *most* possible universes. Physicist Victor Stenger, for one, denied this, and backed it up with several studies, including one he himself undertook, which looked at the consequences of varying several of the supposedly fine-tuned physical quantities simultaneously.[148] Stenger even created a computer program that randomly creates virtual universes in this way, and he claimed that most resulting worlds are compatible with the existence of planets.[149] In the second place, even in universes incapable of supporting biological systems there could be beings "created in God's image." Theists believe that minds are non-physical, or at the very least that it is possible for there to be non-physical minds. After all, God himself is a non-physical, purely spiritual entity. It follows that it is possible for God to create immaterial beings fully capable of having a relationship with him. And if a being is immaterial, then it can exist in any kind of universe whatsoever. The nature of the physical world is therefore irrelevant. In fact, this objection can be taken even further.

God is presumably interested in creating, not mere biological life, but consciousness. And consciousness, on the theist view, does not require a physical substratum at all. Why create a physical universe, then? If the point is to ensure the existence of conscious beings, then God could have accomplished that without stars, planets, or anything else physical: consider heaven.

The most serious objections to the fine-tuning argument, however, have to do with the use it makes of the concept of probability. The argument depends on the claim that it was very unlikely for our universe to exist, given that there were countless other possibilities for how things might have turned out. But it has never been explained how the probability involved can be calculated. It is not enough to say that there are x many possible outcomes and therefore the probability of our universe is 1/x. The problem with such a claim is that we don't know that each of the possible outcomes is equally likely. (Consider: If I ask you to pick any number, what are the chances you will say "7"? Well, there is an infinity of numbers for you to choose from, so by the above reasoning, the chances you will say any given one of them should effectively be zero. And yet we know that it is not all that unlikely for you to pick 7. The reason is obvious: not all outcomes are equally probable; small numbers are much more often picked than very large ones.) So at the very least it seems one cannot say what the likelihood of our particular universe is. But it gets even worse. It seems one cannot even make sense of the claim that some probability applies to this case at all – at least not if by "the universe" we mean everything that exists. If there are many universes with conditions varying from one to another, then we can meaningfully talk about the probability that a given universe will have the characteristics we find in ours. But if our universe is all there is we simply cannot do this. In the latter case, the universe has the properties it has, and that is all. By definition, there cannot be anything else that caused it to have these properties as opposed to some others, and so there cannot be any question as to how likely or unlikely these properties were to begin with.

A comparison with more ordinary cases of probability will help to make this point clearer. Consider a standard six-sided die. What does it mean to say that the probability of rolling a three is one in six? Though several answers to this question have been suggested, the most reasonable one is that the die – if it is fair – has a *propensity* to land one sixth of the time on the number three. This is a characteristic that the die has which results from its more basic properties, such as the fact that it has six equal sides. The die, then, is caused by its characteristics to have a probability of one in six of landing on any given side. But the universe, if it is everything, cannot similarly be caused to have a probability of $1/x$ to have the laws and initial conditions that it has, for the simple reason that it is not *caused* at all. For there to be an analogous situation in the case of the universe, there would have to be some propensity for the universe to have one set of laws rather than another *prior to its existence*. And that, where the universe is all that exists or has ever existed, is by definition impossible.

But we're not done yet. Even if we could somehow meaningfully assign a probability here, the fine-tuning argument still wouldn't go through, for at least a couple of reasons. First, if our universe's characteristics are only one set out of many that it might have had, it remains the case that it had to have some set of characteristics or another. And there is no reason to be any more surprised by this set of characteristics than by any other – just as there is no reason to be surprised that some combination of digits turns out to be the winning lottery number. The fine-tuning proponent contrasts our life-permitting universe with all the supposed life-prohibiting ones there might have been, and argues that the chances for our particular universe are very small. But the appropriate comparison is not between the few life-permitting universes on the one hand, and the far more numerous life-prohibiting ones on the other. Rather, as far as this thought experiment goes, all possible universes should be considered equally. The question whether a universe is life-permitting is no more significant than the question whether a universe has any other characteristic. Fine-tuning proponents, as one might expect, specifically deny this. Craig, for instance, maintains that the situation is akin to one in which you are asked to reach inside a bag containing a billion billion billion black marbles and one white marble, and pick one randomly.[150] If you pick the white marble, you should be incredibly surprised. That's certainly true. But why should we treat the characteristic of being life-permitting apart from all others in this way? Why single it out as the one white marble among all those black ones? Suppose that in only a very few of the possible universes do certain particles called zwarks exist. Would a universe containing zwarks thereby require a special explanation, maybe a fine-tuner who happens to like such funny-sounding particles? Obviously not. We could, after all, say this about every single possible universe, since each and every one has *some* unique characteristic or other. Similarly, even if only a few of the possible universes contain life, it does not follow that a universe like that requires some special explanation.

The second reason the argument still doesn't go through is that it ignores Hume's old "who designed God" objection. The proponent of fine-tuning forgets about the question of God's own characteristics. If it makes sense to ask how likely it is for there to be a universe with properties that permit life, then why doesn't it also make sense to ask how likely it is that there is a God who wants to create such a universe? Why should this God be any more probable than our universe to begin with – or for that matter, than some cosmos-creating entity that produces worlds containing zwarks? For all of these reasons, the idea of fine tuning cannot be taken seriously as an objection to atheism. It just doesn't work.

The cosmological and design arguments, particularly in the versions presented here, are easily the most plausible ones on the side of theism. The Kalam argument is at least as strong as any cosmological argument that has ever been proposed, and the concept of fine tuning presents a greater apparent challenge to atheism than anything else currently on offer. And yet, as we've seen in this chapter, neither of them succeeds. In fact, neither even so much as comes close. There just are no good reasons for believing in a God.

But, as already mentioned, there are in addition reasons for positively *disbelieving* in a God – and not just in the traditional God of most theists. These reasons are presented in the final chapter.

7

THE NONEXISTENCE

OF GOD

Ethiopians have gods that are flat-nosed and dark;
Thracians have gods that are blue-eyed and red-
haired. If cattle and horses... were able to draw
with their hands and do the same things as men,
horses would draw the forms of gods like horses,
and cattle like cattle, and they would make the
gods' bodies the same shape as their own.

– Xenophanes

The ancient Greek philosopher Xenophanes of Colophon,
who lived during the sixth and early fifth centuries BCE, is
remembered for a couple of his observations in particular.
He is known for his conjecture that, since seashells can be
found embedded in the soil on top of mountains many
miles from the ocean, the mountains must have once been
under water – an idea that took over two thousand years

before it became widely accepted; and he is famous for pointing out the human tendency to create gods in our own image. The latter was intended merely as a criticism of the polytheistic religions of his day: the gods were human in shape, and that, Xenophanes rightly thought, was absurd. His criticism can, however, be generalized and taken further. The gods, including the God of monotheism, are a projection of us, but not just in a superficial, physical sense. They are, more importantly, a projection of our *minds*. Gods are modeled, at least in part, on what we intuitively take our minds to be — on what one might call the "common sense" view about the mind.

This common sense view holds that our conscious states are to a great extent independent of the rest of the world. As some psychologists have put it, we are all natural-born dualists, instinctively separating the mental from the physical. Thoughts and emotions do not feel at all like the events that go on around us, outside the mind. Mental states therefore appear to be set apart, to belong in a category of their own. In a word, they appear to be nonphysical. One aspect of this intuition is the feeling that our minds can be disconnected from our bodies — and thus that they might continue existing after death, and maybe even occupy a different realm. As common as the belief in the immateriality of the mind or soul is, however, a second component of the common sense view — the intuition that we have free will — is if anything even harder to shake. After all, to introspection, our decisions seem to come out of nowhere, as if they were uncaused. Even when we go through a lengthy process of deliberation, carefully weighing all the pros and cons prior to choosing some course of action, in the end it feels like we could just as easily have decided to do something else. Most of us therefore suppose that we fully determine whatever we choose to do. As a result, we see ourselves, not merely as another part of existence, but as special entities who introduce novelty into the world in a way that mere objects, and maybe even other animals, cannot. According to this way of thinking, then, our actions are not determined by what happened before, but are instead entirely up to us. This in turn implies that our will is not subject to law – and if it is not subject to law, then it is independent of the physical world, and has power over it.

Although these two beliefs – the immateriality of the mind and freedom of the will – do not necessarily have to go together, they are closely related. After all, it is easier to believe that the mind is free if it is nonphysical, for otherwise it presumably would work in accordance with the laws that govern mere matter. And for the most part, anyone who accepts one of these beliefs also accepts the other. In fact, the majority of people accept both, which is why I'm referring to it as the common sense view.

This way of understanding the mind has also – as I've already alluded to – played a significant role in the development of religious belief, and particularly in how gods are thought of. In what follows, we therefore examine the two constituents of the common sense view, beginning with the question whether the mind is nonphysical and independent of the brain. Our overall investigation, as we will see, leads to the conclusion that God definitely does not exist.

MINDS AND BRAINS

Strictly speaking, the main issue that concerns us here is not whether dualism or its principal philosophical competitor, materialism, is true. Rather, our main concern is a related but nevertheless distinct question: whether mental states depend on the brain in such a way that without the latter, the former would not exist. This is an important issue especially because, if our minds are separate from our physical selves and can survive on their own, then that shows that consciousness does not require a physical substratum in order to function – and that in turn makes the possibility of a nonphysical God far more palatable. If, on the other hand, our minds, and all the other minds that we are familiar with, necessitate a complex central nervous system – if they cannot exist apart from matter – then that greatly reduces the likelihood of disembodied souls, and therefore the likelihood of a purely spiritual being.

When one mentions the hypothesis that the mind is dependent on the brain, most people immediately think of materialism. However, materialism is not the only theory that makes such a claim; it is merely the simplest and most common one that does so. In what follows, then, I won't be specifically arguing for materialism, even though I believe it is correct. I won't be making a distinction between materialism and other views that imply mental states require matter in order to exist: for our purposes, there simply is no reason to go into that much detail. All we need to be concerned with is the debate between those who hold that the mind is dependent upon the physical and those who suppose that it can exist on its own.

The latter view, since it is the one the majority of people accept, can be called "popular dualism." It maintains that, in addition to material substance – which is what rocks, trees, and brains are made of – there is an immaterial substance out of which our minds or souls or spirits are composed, and furthermore that the entities made of this substance can exist independently of anything physical. Proponents of this view accept the existence of an afterlife – and sometimes of a pre-life as well. (It should be pointed out that souls or spirits are essentially the same things as nonphysical minds, even though they are often distinguished from the latter. Believers who insist that it is the soul or spirit *rather than* the mind that survives bodily death, but who also hold that in the afterlife one will experience things, are simply being inconsistent: in order to experience anything, one must have a mind.) Now, there are two main possibilities as far as the afterlife is concerned. The first is that of disembodied existence, which is what we find in the case of ghosts. People who have had near-death experiences sometimes claim leaving their bodies and "hovering" over their physical selves. If their claim is correct, it means – though the term isn't normally used in that context – that they have temporarily become ghosts. Likewise, the departed who are in heaven, hell, purgatory or limbo (when it was still open for business), are, if nonphysical, essentially ghosts dwelling in another realm. The other main type of afterlife is reincarnation. Though this term is usually associated only with Eastern religions (in which most individuals supposedly undergo the process repeatedly) reincarnation is in fact part of the traditional Christian view as well, for that is what the resurrection of the body really amounts to: after we die, we are born again inside a new body – even if this new body has some unusual properties, such as being immortal. Both with disembodied existence and with reincarnation (at least as the latter is understood by the religious), the mind is something that sometimes exists apart from the brain; in the case of reincarnation, this occurs whenever a soul travels from one body to another.

There are three principal arguments against popular dualism. The first – which is also an argument specifically for materialism – begins with the observation that every physical effect, so far as we can see, has a physical cause. This, of course, includes events that happen in the brain. Whatever it is that your neurons are doing at any given moment, they are doing as a result of some prior physical event, such as a signal arriving from a sensory organ. But if everything your neurons do is the result of other physical events, what room is left for an immaterial mind? What can it possibly contribute? That is, if your action of, say, getting up and stretching your legs follows from some neural activity which preceded the act, what do mental events such as your desire to get up – assuming they are nonphysical – have to do with it? The neural activity is a sufficient cause, all by itself, of your getting up. The desire to do so, then, appears superfluous. Thoughts like these have even led some dualists to adopt the view – known as epiphenomenalism – that the mind is utterly ineffectual and powerless; that, in other words, it does not *cause* anything. The mind, according to this theory, is a mere bystander. For example, when you are hungry, you (reasonably enough) suppose that the feeling of hunger is the cause of your acting so as to acquire food. It is what makes you pull into the drive-thru and order a burger and fries. According to epiphenomenalism, however, that is not the case. You are caused to behave as you do by the purely physical events in your brain. The feeling of hunger, being separate from those events, doesn't play a role at all. It merely goes along for the ride. But epiphenomenalism, though it still has its proponents, is hard to accept. Moreover, it can easily be avoided if we say that the feeling of hunger is *the same thing as* the neural activity in your brain that occurs whenever you feel hungry – which is what materialism states.

Evolution provides a second reason to doubt popular dualism – a fact which I'm sure will be regarded by creationists as yet another strike against Darwin. Ever since *The Origin of Species* was published, religious individuals have worried over its implication that we are mere animals – glorified apes – and thus that there is really nothing special or unique about us. The concept of a distinctly human soul is much harder to accept if we grant our simian origins. The current argument is a variation on this basic idea. It is also a fairly simple argument. It begins with the observation that human beings and other higher life forms are descended from creatures that lack minds. If we travel sufficiently far down the evolutionary tree, we eventually reach ancestors of ours that have no mental states of any kind – bacteria, for instance. And if that fact is doubted (maybe some will say that for all we know bacteria are conscious) it doesn't matter, for if we go back even further we reach non-life (after all, life originated from non-living matter), and surely that is unconscious.* Minds, then, appeared on the scene at some point. But how did that happen? If minds are dependent on physical phenomena, that question is relatively easy to answer: they appeared as a result of the increasing complexity of life. Nervous systems became more and more intricate, eventually reaching the level of the human brain. If minds are nonphysical entities, however, the entire thing is far

---

* Though amazingly, not everyone agrees even with that. Some dualists, because they regard consciousness as one of the basic properties in the universe, argue that perhaps everything possesses it – including even such things as electrons.

more mysterious. Where did the immaterial substance out of which minds are composed come from, and how did it attach itself to the nervous systems of organisms? Was the nonphysical stuff always there, ever since the big bang, only perhaps not yet organized into minds? Or did it come into being as a result of later material processes? And how might we ever find out?

The same basic argument can also be made without resorting to evolution. In the womb, a human being develops from a single fertilized egg by the purely physical process of cell division; nothing more than increasing complexity is involved. So once again, where along this process does the immaterial mind enter the scene, and how? Religionists will no doubt insist that God creates a soul, which is then somehow connected (perhaps by industrious angels) to the developing embryo – but they might not be as quick to say the same thing with respect to lower creatures, such as donkeys or snakes. And yet we must remember that they, too, have minds. They are, after all, conscious beings who see, hear, and feel things. Even most invertebrates would have to have souls of some sort.

A third argument against popular dualism, and for our purposes the most significant one, is the so-called argument from neural dependence. Consider people who suffer from Alzheimer's. Because of what is a physical condition – Alzheimer's is, after all, something that affects the brain – they lose a large part of their mental lives. They often reach a state where they are no longer capable of recognizing even their loved ones. But if the mind can function just fine without the brain, why should it be affected in such a way by what turns out to be a mere *neurological* disorder? On the popular dualist view, the brain is at most a means for the nonphysical mind to communicate with the rest of the body. That, at any rate, is what the view implies, even if most popular dualists are unaware of this. According to their theory, the mind receives information from the body (for instance, images and sounds picked up by our sensory organs) and in turn sends signals to it (e.g., the decision to walk or to speak); the brain is only an intermediary. If something happens to the brain, one would expect that communication to be interfered with; the person might no longer be able to control their body, and conversely their body might no longer be able to transmit information to their mind. The mind, however, being distinct and separable from the brain, should otherwise remain unaffected. But that is not what's going on in the case of Alzheimer's. People suffering from the disease are not merely detached from their physical selves; they actually lose many of their purely mental capacities. And of course it is not just with this disease that we find something like this to be the case. People in comas present another problem for popular dualism, as does anyone who receives a sharp blow to the head and temporarily loses consciousness, or for that matter anyone under general anesthesia. And there are many other disorders of the mind that can be traced to disorders of the brain. As medical knowledge increases, more and more physiological causes continue to be discovered. Even such things as depression are now known to have a physical basis.

Consider, too, what happens when someone gets drunk. Again, it is not just the brain that is affected; it is the mind. Someone can lose their ability to think coherently, lose consciousness, or perhaps even do something embarrassing as a result of alcohol in their system. None of this is what one would expect given popular dualism. Alcohol, being a chemical, cannot pass from the bloodstream to the nonphysical realm in order to directly affect the immaterial mind. The mind, therefore, should not feel the impact of excessive drinking. Though an individual might have a hard time driving, walking, and even speaking (because the communication between mind and body – and thus his perceptions and motor functions – might be affected), internally he should remain as clearheaded when plastered as when completely sober. But as I can tell you from personal experience, that's not at all the case.

An even stronger argument along these lines can be made by considering the afterlife. According to popular dualism, the mind survives the death of the brain. But now consider Alzheimer's once again. Those who suffer from it no longer have normal mental states. Often, their loved ones describe them as not really being there anymore – which in advanced cases of the disease is in a sense correct. But then once they die, what happens? Presumably, they get their minds back – and if so, the question that must be asked is, where were their minds in the meantime? More importantly, why should we suppose that minds can be nearly destroyed by a disease that affects the brain and yet survive the *complete annihilation* of the brain that occurs at death? That makes very little sense indeed.

All of the above argues against the possibility of disembodied minds. And if something physical is required for there to be minds of any sort, then theism – which involves belief in the existence of a nonphysical being – is ruled out. Now, one must be careful here. It could be that *our* minds depend on our brains, but that the same cannot be said of God's mind. But all that means is that the above arguments, even if successful, do not conclusively disprove the existence of God. That, however, is not what they were meant to do. Rather, these arguments present evidence against belief in God – and rather strong evidence at that. One may talk about the *possibility* that there are conscious immaterial beings somewhere, but the fact remains that all the information we have points toward minds being dependent on some physical substratum. Every single mind we are aware of is like that. We therefore have good reasons here against believing in God.

There are, of course, arguments supporting the popular dualist view as well, and one cannot make a thorough case against it without considering them. In the next section we will therefore examine the strongest evidence for this opposing view. As we will see, though, it is not sufficient to undermine the above conclusions.

NEAR-DEATH EXPERIENCES

Other than religion, the main reason in favor of the dualist view as far as most people are concerned consists of empirical evidence suggesting the existence of disembodied spirits. A hundred years ago, this evidence came mostly from séances, in which mediums claimed to make contact with the departed, and which for a while were all the rage. But as more and more of these mediums were exposed as frauds, the fad passed, and today it is about as dead as the people who were supposedly communicating from the other side. It has been replaced, however, by something that at first sight appears to provide much stronger confirmation than séances ever offered: that of near-death experiences, or NDEs. Many individuals who have been close to death, particularly those who find themselves undergoing certain life-saving medical procedures, have reported such experiences.

The details are admittedly intriguing. The most common features reported by individuals who have had an NDE are feelings of peace, out-of-body sensations, and – perhaps most fascinating of all – the feeling that one is moving along a dark tunnel toward a bright light. (This light is most often white or pale yellow, but can be almost any other color: green, red, purple and blue have all been reported.) Often, subjects also tell of entering this light, which they often describe as brighter than anything they have ever seen – but which, they often also say, does not at all hurt their eyes. Sometimes dead family members or even religious figures are seen as well. NDEs have been reported since ancient times, by people of all faiths, and by children as well as by adults. Nor is it by any means only the religious who claim to have them: the eminent philosopher A. J. Ayer, an outspoken atheist, famously had such an experience as well.

NDEs are obviously suggestive of certain religious beliefs (though it may be that, at least in some cases, the NDEs were themselves the cause of such beliefs; for example, someone in ancient times reporting an out-of-body experience might have been thought by others to have actually exited their physical self, leading them to conclude that one's soul can in fact carry on an independent existence). What must be ascertained is whether the experiences are more than mere illusions – whether they in fact provide good evidence for an immaterial self. And the answer to that question is, unfortunately, no.

The first thing to note is that the incidents in question are by no means limited to near-death situations. Out-of-body experiences are sometimes caused in cases of extreme tiredness or stress. Military pilots training in centrifuges, where they are exposed to g-forces that induce loss of consciousness, regularly undergo not just out-of-body experiences but the tunnel effect and a sense of serenity and euphoria as well. Individuals in sensory deprivation experiments sometimes also report such episodes. In addition, all of the effects associated with NDEs are common drug-induced hallucinations. Ether, for example, often creates the tunnel effect at doses in which the subject is not in any danger of dying.

A particularly suggestive case, reported in the scientific journal *Nature* in 2002, involved electrical stimulation of the brain of a woman suffering from severe epileptic seizures. The neuroscientists working with this patient discovered that they were able to induce out-of-body experiences in her at will, and that the intensity of the experiences was related to the level of stimulation. More amazingly, the height at which the patient felt she was floating above her body was directly related to the amount of electrical current involved.[151]

As is the case with most things about the brain, neuroscientists are still working on the details as to what is going on during such experiences. However, some things are beginning to be understood. For instance, there is some evidence that the tunnel effect is created in the visual cortex (the part of the brain responsible for vision) as a result of what psychologist Susan Blackmore calls "disinhibition" of the brain cells – meaning that "a lot of cells that should not be firing [because the brain is not receiving visual data]... start to fire."[152] These cells are concentrated toward the center of the visual field, so that when they start firing randomly, many more will be in the middle, producing the sensation of a bright light surrounded by darkness. As the effect increases, the area of bright light does as well, and Blackmore theorizes that it is this that produces the sensation of moving down the tunnel toward the light: the bright area gets progressively larger and thus appears to be getting closer. At its greatest extent, the whole visual field is lit up, creating the appearance that one has finally left the tunnel and entered the light. Moreover, the whole thing will appear exceedingly bright without, however, affecting one's eyes – for the simple reason that one's eyes are not in any way involved; the entire event takes place in the brain.

The feelings of peace and well-being that are also commonly reported are, if anything, actually easier to account for. In situations involving serious danger and severe stress, the brain releases endorphins, chemicals which have a calming effect and in extreme cases may even bring about the sensation of great bliss. Other naturally occurring neurotransmitters, such as serotonin and dopamine, also appear to be involved. Blackmore mentions a famous study made of people who had nearly died in mountaineering accidents. One might imagine that, as they were falling, these individuals would experience terrible fear and desperation, but that is not the case: they instead described being calm and very accepting of their situation. Naturally occurring brain chemicals can also cause one to have hallucinations, in the same way as certain drugs do. Individuals who have had an NDE and talked with Jesus quite understandably regard their experience as life-altering. Anyone considering such things objectively, however, is more likely to be struck by the fact that religious figures reported in NDEs, besides being relatively rare, are always specific to individuals' religions. As Blackmore points out, there has never been a Hindu who saw Jesus, nor a Christian who saw a Hindu god.[153] In addition, the "beings of light" have in some cases been identified by the patient afterwards as the medical staff present during the procedure.[154] Furthermore, children are more likely to see living friends than dead relatives, which doesn't fit in with the hypothesis that the experience is of a world beyond.[155] And the experience reported by Ayer, the atheist philosopher mentioned above, seems to be the sort of thing only a philosopher's subconscious would invent: in it, Ayer wrote, there were creatures who were in charge of space – only they had not done their job right, and as a consequence space had become "slightly out of joint." Moreover, the laws of nature had as a result "ceased to function as they should," and Ayer felt that it was up to him to "put things right."[156] Experiences like this suggest ordinary dreams more than they do the afterlife.

Another popular belief is that individuals who have had out-of-body experiences describe things they could not possibly have known without actually leaving their bodies. However, in spite of numerous sensationalist claims, not one such case has ever been shown to have occurred. One particularly interesting example that Blackmore mentions involved a patient who, in an account given in a book on NDEs, supposedly reported seeing such things as "the color of the sheets covering the operating table, the hairstyle of the head scrub nurse, ... and even the trivial fact that her anesthesiologist that day was wearing unmatched socks." But what made this case truly amazing is that, according to the author who told the story, the patient – a woman named Sarah – had been blind from birth! How could a blind person report such things unless out-of-body experiences are veridical? Blackmore, understandably intrigued and wishing to get more details about this Sarah, wrote the author in order to see if she could contact the patient herself. The author admitted there was no Sarah! She was, he claimed, a "composite" of different cases. He went on to explain that "the 'fact' that

Sarah was congenitally blind was a way of illustrating that non-local ways of gaining information bypass the senses and are ultimately independent of the brain." Blackmore followed up on the cases that "Sarah" was supposedly based on but was unable to find even one involving a blind person who provided an accurate account of anything.[157] And even sighted individuals have never been shown to do any better. In a three-year study begun in 2008, pictures were hung face-up from ceilings in hospital operating rooms in the hope that those having out-of-body experiences might describe their content. In terms of identifying the pictures, no positive results were reported.[158]

For all that has been said, it *could* of course still be the case that NDEs are actual experiences of the afterlife. On the other hand, they may have purely physical explanations; they might be nothing more than hallucinations created in the brain under certain unusual conditions. And, as much as we'd prefer it to be otherwise, given the evidence in favor of the mind's dependence on the brain, the latter possibility is by far the more likely.

The conclusion one should draw from all this is that minds are almost certainly produced by complex physical systems such as the human brain and therefore cannot exist apart from matter. As already pointed out, this means that the existence of a non-physical God is at best highly improbable. There is an even stronger reason for rejecting theism, however. So far, we have covered only the first of the two essential beliefs that comprise the common sense view about the mind. The second, the belief in free will, is even more important for our purposes. For, as we will see in the next section, its inherent problems provide us with a complete refutation of the theistic worldview. The argument that follows, then, is the principal one in support of atheism, and therefore the most important one in this book.

WHY THERE DEFINITELY IS NO GOD

Theism is to some extent the result of a primitive and outdated view regarding the nature of causation – for it is in part because human beings first thought of causes in terms of the decisions of conscious agents that deities were invented. Gods are unseen agents that we assume are responsible for events which we cannot otherwise explain. Storms, volcanoes, the changing of the seasons – all these things are outside human control, and to primitive minds it was therefore natural to suppose that they were brought about by more powerful versions of themselves. Moreover, since gods are modeled on us, they are thought to cause things in essentially the same way that we supposedly do: namely, by freely deciding to do so. We appear to be able to initiate chains of causation, and deities are likewise understood as "causal initiators." That is why when a god is appealed to as the reason for something, he is thought of as the *ultimate* reason for it. It is not as if he himself was in any way made to bring about the result in question; it was entirely up to him. Contrast this with a scientific explanation of an event. If a tsunami occurs, seismologists may inform us that the reason for it was an earthquake. But of course the earthquake itself has a cause: it may have occurred as a result of the movement of plates in the earth's crust – and that in turn has a cause, and so on. If an angry god is responsible for the tsunami, however, the buck stops with him. True, his anger will have some explanation, as does the anger of a human being. But the *decision* to send the tsunami is solely that god's to make; angry or not, he could have decided differently. Gods are the sole authors of their actions.

The concept of a god, then, is, when properly understood, the concept of a being with free will – and more precisely, with the kind of freedom that allows decisions to come out of nowhere, as it were. Only then can the actions of a god be both volitional and independent of the laws that govern the rest of reality; only then can these actions be the ultimate reason for the existence of something else. Gods are the uncaused causes of the effects they produce.

This doesn't mean that someone absolutely cannot use the word "god" for something lacking free will. The term has been used in ways that stretch its original meaning beyond recognition. As I've previously mentioned, some use "God" to refer to such things as the laws of nature, or the moral principles that the universe supposedly exhibits, or even something more abstract – things that fail to capture what ordinary people mean by a deity. Similarly, it is possible for someone to apply the term "gods" to entities in a way inconsistent with the above. One example is found in the philosophy of some of the ancient Greek atomists, who argued that if there are gods, they are physical beings who, like everything else, behave in accordance with the deterministic laws of our universe. But such beings – mortal entities made of atoms and subject to the laws of cause and effect – would be more akin to powerful alien creatures than to genuine gods; they could not be thought of as the ultimate explanation for any fact about the universe.

Gods, then, in the proper sense of the word, *have* to be free – and in that respect, they are actually different from mere human beings. Most of us believe we have free will, but that doesn't mean free will is a necessary component of what makes someone human. There are other characteristics that are sufficient to make us members of our species even without metaphysical freedom. It follows that it is not fatal to our concept of ourselves to abandon belief in free will. Gods, on the other hand, are necessarily free because they serve as ultimate explanations, and thus as causal starting points, for other phenomena. A god that isn't free isn't really a god.

But now here's the problem: this kind of freedom – what philosophers call libertarian free will – is, as will be shown below, impossible. It's not just that human beings lack freedom of the will, as many have argued. The problem goes much deeper than that: it's that the concept of free will is actually an incoherent one. The kind of freedom most of us believe in (and even take for granted) is a logical impossibility. And yet that is what an entity would *have to* have in order to qualify as a god. It follows that God cannot exist. And not just the monotheistic God, of course: the claim applies to all gods. Thus, we can say that none of the deities humans have ever believed in – whether it be Zeus, Mithra, Isis, Yahweh, Vishnu, or any of the thousands of others – are possible. Their existence is no more allowed than the existence of round squares or of married bachelors. What we have here, then, is a refutation of every genuine type of theism.

But why claim such a thing regarding free will? On what basis am I arguing that it is impossible? After all, that we are free is something that appears obvious to almost everyone. It certainly *feels* as if our decisions are free – that anything we do intentionally is entirely up to us, and for that reason might not have been done. Think of any action you have performed deliberately: it no doubt seems to you that you could have decided differently, that you could have done something else instead. Up until the very moment you made a decision, it was still an open question what you would do, and it could have gone either way; the choice was yours and yours alone.

This is one of the common reasons offered in favor of free will. There is another popular one: most people also insist on the reality of free will because they regard it as essential for morality. After all, if there is no free will, then what we do is in some ultimate sense not up to us – and if that is the case, how can we be held accountable for our actions? This second argument, then, is that, since we are morally responsible for our actions, free will exists – or at the very least, since it is *preferable* to think of ourselves as morally responsible, it is preferable to believe in free will.

These reasons for accepting free will are at best inconclusive, however. To begin with, the mere feeling that one is free doesn't really prove anything. It is in fact what we should expect given that we are not conscious of the underlying mechanisms at work in the brain. As new atheist and neuroscientist Sam Harris points out in his book *Free Will* – and others have previously made the same claim – we simply do not experience all of the causes that factor into the decisions we make. The intuition that we are free, then, can certainly be an illusion; it is not a good enough reason for believing in metaphysical freedom. And obviously one cannot rewind time to the moment at which a given decision was made in order to have a second go at it and test whether one could really have done otherwise.

As to the second argument: even if free will is necessary for moral responsibility, that of course does not prove free will exists. For in that case, it might instead mean that moral responsibility is an illusion as well. And that is precisely what many who dispute the existence of metaphysical freedom – from celebrated attorney

Clarence Darrow to Sam Harris himself – have concluded. There is, however, a real question whether as a practical matter we can abandon the concept of moral responsibility, and whether it would be a good thing if we did. On such a view, not only should we stop considering criminals morally responsible for their crimes; we should also stop thinking of anyone as deserving praise for good deeds. Rewards and punishments would still serve the purpose of encouraging some behaviors and discouraging others, and thus would still be justified as *means* to an end, but neither would be justified as ends in themselves. Murderers and rapists could no more be regarded as evil than hurricanes or tornados can. And that's a difficult notion to accept.

Fortunately, there is another solution. Although I won't defend it here, as it would take us too far off our main topic, there is the view called compatibilism (accepted by, among others, the philosopher Daniel Dennett, who is also one of the principal new atheists), and this view maintains that the kind of free will we have been discussing – the freedom to choose from among different possible courses of action – is not necessary for moral responsibility after all. Thus, in denying the existence of free will as that term is usually understood, I am not implying that we shouldn't hold individuals accountable for their actions. There is still a moral distinction to be made between human beings, who understand the consequences of what they do, and inanimate processes – or even non-human animals – that do not.

So much for the arguments in favor of free will; we still need to consider the principal one against it, the argument which states that such freedom simply cannot exist. To understand that argument, however, we must first examine the nature of free will. What does it really mean to say that we are free?

The first thing to note is that free will (the kind under consideration here) is incompatible with determinism. If determinism is true, there is only one possible future, only one way things can turn out. And in that case, we cannot choose from among more than one possible course of action; we can only do what the laws of cause and effect dictate we do. Remember, the type of freedom we are discussing here requires that there be genuine alternatives available for us to choose from. But if there is only one possible way the future can turn out, then no real alternatives exist. Free actions, then, cannot be completely caused by what happened before. This is the reason determinism is regarded as such a controversial doctrine: it rules out the kind of freedom that most people believe in.

It isn't just determinism that is incompatible with free will, however. Randomness, or chance, is also inconsistent with it. That is, if an action of yours is ultimately the result of chance — if there is no reason why that action as opposed to some other was performed — then it isn't free either. For in that case, it is not true that it was up to you to perform the action; it is something that happened by accident, as it were. If something *just happens* in your brain that causes you to perform some act, then your behavior certainly isn't free. Randomness is just as much an obstacle to freedom as determinism is.

A free act, then, is one that is neither determined nor random. It follows that in order for free will to exist, there must be a third category of events lying between those that are the result of what happened before and those that are ultimately a matter of chance. Free acts belong in a class unto themselves. And therein lies the problem, for, as it turns out, there is no such third category, nor can there be one. The determined and the random cover the entire range of possibilities. Thus, there is no room for free will; it is a metaphysical impossibility.

We can see that this is the case by thinking about the events leading up to the exact moment when a decision is reached. Consider, for example, Lee Harvey Oswald's fateful decision to pull the trigger and take that first shot on November 22, 1963. Like all human behavior, this event originated with the firing of certain neurons in the agent's brain. Now, if causal determinism is true, these neurons fired because of the conditions that were present immediately before, while those conditions in turn were the result of previous events, and so on, like a line of dominoes extending into the infinite past. And like the toppling of the last domino in the series, the end result was inevitable. Oswald could not have decided to do otherwise. If determinism is true, then any given decision derives from the events that led up to it and therefore cannot be avoided. But what if determinism isn't true? In that case, even if everything happened exactly as before, Oswald might have decided differently. It is as if every domino fell as expected but the last one remained standing. But now the question that arises is whether Oswald's decision in this second scenario could be anything other than a random one.

Above, I mentioned the notion of rewinding time back to the moment a decision was reached. Now, even though such a thing of course cannot be done, it does make for a good thought experiment – an instructive way to think about what's actually involved. If determinism is true, and one were to rewind time to the moment before Oswald decided to pull the trigger, the result would obviously be the same: he would once again proceed with the assassination. That is, with everything exactly the same, the end result would necessarily be the same as well. If, however, *in*determinism is true, then it is possible that the second time around Oswald would lose his nerve (say) and not fire. Suppose, then, that that is what happens. Suppose, in other words, that we rewind time to the moment Oswald is about to make his decision and that this time he does not fire his gun. Everything up to the previous moment is exactly as it was the first time around. Oswald finds himself in the exact same surroundings: he sees the same scene unfolding in front of him, he hears the same sounds and feels the same things as before. Furthermore, everything is precisely identical with Oswald himself: he has the same memories, the same feelings, and the same beliefs. The pattern of neurons that has just fired in his brain is the one that fired in his brain the first time around. And yet, at the last moment, in spite of everything being exactly the same, he decides not to pull the trigger. What could possibly explain the difference? What could make his new decision anything other than random?

The believer in free will wants to claim that there is a reason why Oswald decided as he did, for it was a conscious act of will on his part. However, to have a reason is to find something in the overall situation that leads one to make a particular choice. If the overall situation one finds oneself in does not lead to a particular decision – *if under precisely identical conditions one's decision could have been different* – then the actual decision cannot be based solely on it. But in our thought experiment, Oswald finds himself in the exact same circumstances as before, yet decides differently. The circumstances he finds himself in, then, are not what the decision is ultimately based on. If they were, his decision would have to be the same both times. But the overall situation is all there is; it covers every possible factor involved. Aside from it, there is nothing left for the decision to be based on, nothing that explains why *that* decision, as opposed to some other one, was reached. And in that case, the decision cannot be anything other than random. It's as if at the crucial moment Oswald simply flipped a coin in his mind.

It is important to realize that, although I have presented things in terms of neural events occurring in a brain, this argument in no way depends on materialism, or anything similar, being true. The exact same point can be made (even if somewhat less clearly, due to a lack of specifics) with reference to a non-physical mind. That is, if Oswald's action originates in his immaterial mind, it nevertheless remains the case that his mind must operate either entirely deterministically or to some extent randomly. The point being made applies to any entity whatsoever, whether physical or not, for it is a *logical* point – namely, that there are only two possibilities as far as why any action is performed (or why any event at all occurs, for that matter). Either the action is the result of the overall situation in which it is performed, so that, given the situation, it *had to* occur, or it is not the result of the overall situation. If it is not the result of the overall situation, then under those exact same conditions it might not have been performed. But if the action could have failed to take place under the exact same conditions then its occurrence is ultimately random. Therefore, the only two possibilities are determinism and randomness – which of course leaves no room for freedom. It appears, then, that free will is a logical impossibility; as claimed above, the concept itself is incoherent.

And this means God is ruled out as well. God is not merely a projection of us as human beings; he is modeled on a particular understanding we have of ourselves. He is based on the intuition that the mind is inherently free and independent of the world around us. But as we have just seen, this kind of freedom cannot exist. And of course if beings require such freedom in order to qualify as gods, then gods, too, cannot exist. They are impossible. We can therefore conclude that there definitely is no God.

It is important to understand exactly what is being claimed here. Most atheists maintain that one cannot prove that there are no gods. As they often put it, "one cannot prove a negative." Actually, one *can* prove a negative, and I wish people would stop saying one can't – but what they mean is that it is usually difficult, if not impossible, to prove the nonexistence of something. As I admitted in the first chapter, I cannot prove that there has never been a unicorn: I would have to have looked everywhere and throughout the entirety of the earth's history to conclusively rule out the existence of these creatures. Similarly, it is widely held, one cannot prove that, say, Zeus does not exist. This does not mean it might be reasonable to believe in Zeus: not only is there no evidence for such a being, there is indirect evidence against his existence (based on what we know about humans and their mythmaking tendencies, for instance). But this, it is usually thought, is as far as one can go in one's denial of Zeus.

Now, I am claiming that in fact Zeus cannot possibly be real, and that therefore we can be certain of his nonexistence. This denial, however, depends on taking seriously the claim that Zeus is a god; it does not rule out some being *called* Zeus who is not free-willed. Such a being, however, would – as has already been pointed out –

be more akin to a powerful alien creature than to a god: he would not be above the laws of nature, nor could he be regarded as the ultimate explanation for the occurrence of any natural event. Zeus — the being that the ancient Greeks believed in, who they understood as ultimately responsible for thunderbolts and for many other things — *that* being definitely does not exist.

This argument against the existence of gods is likely to be doubly controversial. Not only does it claim that God cannot exist — a stronger claim than is usually made by atheists — it in addition bases this conclusion on a rejection of something else people find difficult to abandon, our supposed freedom. The difficulties for the concept of freedom on which the argument depends, however, have been pointed out by numerous philosophers, and I for one do not see any way around them. Philosophers who continue to maintain that there is such a thing as free will (in our sense of the term) have never been able to present a plausible or even clear account of the concept they have in mind. The conclusion, then, appears to be inescapable. If, as I maintain, a being must have the kind of metaphysical freedom described in order to qualify as a deity, and if such freedom is impossible, then there cannot be any deities, period. The truth about God is that he does not *and cannot* exist. Atheism isn't merely true; it is *necessarily* true.

CONCLUSION: A WORLD WITHOUT GOD

Most people are understandably reluctant to abandon belief in God. Perhaps they fear that they cannot live without such a belief, or even that life would be barren and meaningless if not for their religious commitments. They may also feel uneasy questioning fundamental views that they have accepted all of their lives. It is always easier, after all, to fall back on familiar ways of thinking. One can usually find comfort in them. It's not that people don't have doubts, of course; many – perhaps most – are less than completely confident about their faith. But they may also be afraid that the dogmas of religion *might* just turn out to be true, and so are hedging their bets. The psychological force of Pascal's Wager – of asking yourself "what if you're wrong?" – should not be underestimated.

People also tend to find the idea that there is no one in control of things – and that our existence is therefore to a great extent haphazard – rather unnerving. The world seems a much safer, much cozier, place if we imagine there being someone in charge – especially someone who supposedly loves us. And yet when one thinks about it, the reassurance provided by belief in God here is actually pretty indefensible. For if there were a God, what we should be asking ourselves is just what kind of God he is. After all, we are confronted with a world in which terrible things happen all of the time, a world in which hunger, disease, wars and natural disasters kill millions of innocent people and make life miserable for countless others. But if that is the universe that a God created, what does that suggest about his attitude toward us? It is common to see those who have suffered the worst kind of tragedy thank God for having escaped with nothing but their lives. They may have lost everything, may even have lost friends and neighbors who weren't so "lucky," yet they praise the Almighty for having miraculously spared *them*. In a way, this is good: it demonstrates the natural resilience of the human animal. But it is also rather sad, for it proves just how irrational our species is. The existence of a God who allows all of the terrible tragedies we see around us should not provide us with much in the way of consolation. That there *isn't* such a God, then, isn't something we should find at all disturbing.

The doctrines specific to individual religions also come up short here. Consider the Christian system. If you believe in Jesus, you undoubtedly suppose that everything will turn out all right, at least for you: as a believer, you will certainly end up in heaven. That, at any rate, seems to be the attitude of the majority of Christians (and explains why so many people are followers of Jesus). But what about the fact that many with different religious views, including even some Christians from other denominations, believe just as ardently that you are destined for hell? Protestants sometimes regard Catholicism as a cult that does not represent real Christianity, while Catholics in some cases consider membership in their "one true church" the only path to salvation. Muslims, of course, think both are damned – just as many Christians believe all followers of other religions are. Moreover, even if for some unjustifiable reason you are certain that yours is the correct belief, shouldn't you nevertheless feel uneasy about the fate of those others? It cannot really be a good thing that they are going to end up suffering for all eternity, especially when you consider that for the majority their "crime" was nothing more than being unlucky enough to be raised in the wrong tradition. Such a system is inherently unfair. In fact, it is downright immoral. As Christopher Hitchens pointed out, it is nothing less than a "celestial dictatorship."[159] And if that's what it means to have a God, then we are much better off in a godless world. Better to take our chances with an impersonal and entirely physical, but at least neutral, universe than with a cosmic despot who would punish his creatures for failing to worship him in the right way.

Atheists are often accused of a kind of arrogance for supposedly refusing to accept the existence of anything greater than themselves (and comments such as the ones I just made above certainly won't help matters). For many believers, then, the entire debate between the two sides is at least in part a question of humility. Theists are humble servants of their creator, whereas nonbelievers are ingrates who have rebelled against their maker. One can easily turn the tables around, however, and level such a charge of immodesty at theism instead. God, after all, is not merely a human invention; the ruler and supreme entity of this world is also a being created in our own image. On the standard religious view, not only are we the center of the universe – the reason for creation itself – but even more amazingly, a human-like consciousness is believed responsible for the existence of everything else. This makes it very apparent that the concept of a deity has its origin in a kind of human hubris. That's not to say that it is *theists* who are arrogant: I don't mean to imply that the faithful believe because they suppose there must be someone like them in charge of everything. That would be as false a claim as that atheists disbelieve because they do not want there to be something greater than themselves. But humanity in general – all of us, believer and nonbeliever alike – are naturally predisposed to interpret reality through rather narrow anthropomorphic lenses, to see purpose and meaning as part of nature itself and to place ourselves at the center of it all. That is a natural human inclination, and it is only by arriving at a deeper understanding of the world and its workings that such primitive notions can be put behind us. Only then can we rise above our natural simplistic tendencies. Only then can we go beyond the delusion that is theism.

NOTES

[1] Benjamin Fearnow & Mickey Woods, "Richard Dawkins Preaches to Nonbelievers at Reason Rally", *The Atlantic*, March 24, 2012.

[2] John Allen Paulos, "Who's Counting: Distrusting Atheists," ABC News, April 2, 2006, abcnews.go.com/Technology/story?id=1786422&page=1

[3] Jeffrey M. Jones, "Some Americans Reluctant to Vote for Mormon, 72-Year-Old Presidential Candidates," *Gallup*, Feb. 20, 2007, www.gallup.com/poll/26611/Some-Americans-Reluctant-Vote-Mormon-72YearOld-Presidential-Candidates.aspx

[4] Ronald Bailey, "Why Do So Many Believers Think Atheists Are Worse Than Rapists?", *Reason.com*, reason.com/archives/2012/03/27/believers-atheists-worse-rapists

[5] Margaret Downey, "Discrimination Against Atheists - The Facts," *Free Inquiry*, Vol. 24, No. 4, June/July 2004, www.secularhumanism.org/library/fi/downey_24_4.htm

[6] Psalms 14:1 and 53:1 (NRSV)

[7] John 3:18 (NRSV)

[8] Thomas Aquinas, *Summa Theologica*, Part 2, II, Q. 10, A. 3

[9] Lee Strobel, *The Case for Faith*, Zondervan, 2000, p. 222

[10] Dinesh D' Souza, *What's So Great about Christianity*, Regnery Publishing, 2007, pp. 269 and 272

[11] transcripts.cnn.com/TRANSCRIPTS/0701/31/pzn.01.html

[12] Eric Zorn, "No Christian Love Given to Atheist," *Chicago Tribune*, articles.chicagotribune.com/2008-04-06/news/0804050331_1_childhood-obesity-pull-atheist. (Audio of Davis's comments at: www.youtube.com/watch?v=DRwgvzg-wA4)

[13] James S. Spiegel, *The Making of an Atheist*, Moody Publishers, 2010, p. 18

[14] Psalms 14:1 (NRSV)

[15] Lee Strobel, *The Case for Christ*, Zondervan, 1998, p. 13

[16] 2 Corinthians 4:4

[17] Hebrews 11:1

[18] Victor J. Stenger, *The New Atheism*, Prometheus Books, 2009, p. 59.

[19] Quoted in Hector Avalos, "Atheism Was Not the Cause of the Holocaust," in John W. Loftus, ed., *The Christian Delusion*, Prometheus Books, 2010, p. 370.

[20] *Ibid.*, p. 372

[21] Scott Hahn and Benjamin Wiker, *Answering the New Atheism,* Emmaus Road Publishing, 2008, p. 94

[22] Numbers 22:28-30

[23] Gleason L. Archer Jr., *Encyclopedia of Bible Difficulties*, Zondervan, 1982, p. 21

[24] Genesis 2:5 (NRSV)

[25] Genesis 2:18-19

[26] Paul Tobin, "The Bible and Modern Scholarship," in John W. Loftus, ed., *op. cit.*, pp. 149-150

[27] Norman L. Geisler and Thomas Howe, *The Big Book of Bible Difficulties*, Baker Books, 1992, p. 35

[28] Archer, *op. cit.*, pp. 68-69

[29] Leviticus 11:13-19, Deuteronomy 14:11-18

[30] Martin Gardner, *Fads & Fallacies*, Dover Publications, 1957 (1952), pp. 16-19

[31] Plato, *Phaedo*, 110b

[32] Martin Gardner, *op. cit.*, p. 17

[33] 2 Kings 2:23-24

[34] See Mark 2:23-28

[35] Numbers 15: 32-36

[36] Deuteronomy 20:16-18

[37] Exodus 32:29 (NRSV)

[38] Numbers 31:17-18

[39] Bart Ehrman, *God's Problem*, HarperCollins, 2009 (2008), p. 46

[40] Matthew 5:17-19 (NRSV)

[41] Romans 7:6 (NRSV)

[42] Paul Copan, "Are Old Testament Laws Evil?", in William Lane Craig and Chad Meister, eds., *God Is Great, God Is Good*, InterVarsity Press, 2009, p. 138

[43] *Ibid.*, p. 143

[44] Leviticus 19:19

[45] Copan, *op. cit.*, p. 148

[46] *Ibid.*

[47] Archer, *op. cit.*, p. 158

[48] Geisler and Howe, o*p. cit.*, p. 110

[49] Geisler and Howe, *op. cit.*, p. 138

[50] Archer, *op. cit.*, p. 159

[51] See
www.reasonablefaith.org/site/News2?page=NewsArticle&
id=5767

[52] Geisler and Howe, *op. cit.*, p. 138

[53] Hector Avalos, "Yahweh Is a Moral Monster," in John W.
Loftus, ed., *op. cit.*, pp. 224-225

[54] Acts 1:18

[55] Douglas Wilson, *Letter from a Christian Citizen*,
American Vision, 2007, p. 67

[56] *Ibid.*

[57] Matthew 2:22-23 (NRSV)

[58] Luke 2:39, emphasis added

[59] Matthew 2:15

[60] Bart D. Ehrman, *Jesus, Interrupted*, HarperCollins, 2010
(2009), p. 33

[61] 1 Chronicles 3:10-19

[62] See, e.g., Tim Callahan, *Secret Origins of the Bible*,
Millennium Press, 2002, pp. 362-363

[63] Luke 1:1-4 (NRSV)

[64] Bart D. Ehrman, *Misquoting Jesus*, HarperCollins, 2005,
p. 67

65 See *ibid.*, pp. 67-68

66 Matthew 28:7

67 Matthew 28:10 (NRSV)

68 Luke 24:13-15

69 Luke 24:33-51

70 Quoted in Lee Strobel, *The Case for Christ*, p. 217

71 See Ehrman, *op. cit.*, pp. 168-169

72 Richard Bauckham, *Jesus: A Very Short Introduction*, Oxford University Press, 2011, p. 104

73 1 Corinthians 15:5-8

74 Matthew 24:34

75 Luke 9:27

76 See Martin Gardner, "The Wandering Jew and the Second Coming," in *From the Wandering Jew to William F. Buckley Jr.*, Prometheus Books, 2000

77 Matthew 27:45

78 Matthew 27:52-53

79 Martin Gardner, *The Whys of a Philosophical Scrivener*, Quill, 1983, p. 301

[80] Luke 16:28

[81] Matthew 25:41

[82] Matthew 13:42

[83] Revelation 14:10-11

[84] *Mark Twain's Notebooks and Journals, Vol. 3*, University of California Press, 1980

[85] Quoted in Lee Strobel, *The Case for Faith*, p. 245

[86] Georges Rey, "Meta-atheism: Religious Avowal as Self-Deception," in Louise M. Antony, ed., *Philosophers without Gods*, Oxford University Press, 2007, pp. 253-254

[87] 1 Timothy 2:4

[88] Ehrman, o*p. cit.*, pp. 63-65

[89] Acts 17:31-32 (NRSV)

[90] Richard Swinburne, *The Existence of God*, Oxford University Press, 2004 (1979), pp. 211-212

[91] Quoted in Lee Strobel, *The Case for Faith*, p. 263

[92] William Lane Craig, "Theistic Critiques of Atheism," in Michael Martin, ed., *The Cambridge Companion to Atheism*, Cambridge University Press, 2007, p. 71

[93] Alvin Plantinga, *Warranted Christian Belief*, Oxford University Press, 2000, pp. 167-186

[94] Dinesh D'Souza, *What's So Great about God*, Tyndale, 2012. For my review of D'Souza's book, see "What's So Great about Evil?", *Skeptic*, Vol. 19, No. 1, 2014, pp. 61-62

[95] William Lane Craig and Walter Sinnot-Armstrong, *God? A Debate between a Christian and an Atheist*, Oxford University Press, 2004, p. 112

[96] "U.N. Chief: Hunger kills 17,000 kids daily," *CNN*, 17 Nov 2009 edition.cnn.com/2009/WORLD/europe/11/17/italy.food.summit/

[97] C. S. Lewis, *Mere Christianity*, HarperCollins, 2001 (1952), p. 48

[98] See, e.g., 1 John 5:19

[99] Darren Oldriddge, *The Devil: A Very Short Introduction*, Oxford University Press, 2012, pp. 90-91

[100] See Matthew 5:45

[101] Richard Swinburne, *The Existence of God*, p. 264

[102] Richard Dawkins, *The God Delusion*, Houghton Mifflin, 2006, p. 64

[103] www.atheist-experience.com/archive/?y=2004 (video #330)

[104] Dinesh D'Souza, *op. cit.*, Chpt. 7

[105] Lee Strobel, *The Case for Faith*, pp. 46-47.

[106] William Lane Craig and Walter Sinnot-Armstrong, *op. cit.*, pp. 125-126.

[107] Jean-Paul Sartre, *Existentialism and Human Emotions*, Citadel, 1985 (1957), p. 22

[108] Sam Harris, *The Moral Landscape*, Free Press, 2010, p. 5

[109] Allan Bloom, *The Closing of the American Mind*, Touchstone, 1987, p. 25

[110] Gottfried Leibniz, *Discourse on Metaphysics*, section II

[111] Chad Meister, "God, Evil and Morality," in William Lane Craig and Chad Meister, eds., *God Is Great, God Is Good*, p. 112

[112] See, e.g., Stephen D. Unwin, *The Probability of God*, Crown Forum, 2003

[113] Matthew 15:24-26

[114] Sam Harris, "Clarifying the Moral Landscape – A Response to Ryan Born," blog post, Jun 6, 2014

[115] Sam Harris, *The Moral Landscape*, p. 12

[116] *Ibid.*, p. 210 (n. 50). For Nozick's original statement of the thought experiment, see *Anarchy, State, and Utopia*, Basic Books, 1974, p. 41

[117] Harris, *op. cit.*, p. 211 (n. 50)

[118] Karen Musalo, "When Rights and Cultures Collide" at www.scu.edu/ethics/publications/iie/v8n3/rightsandcultures.html

[119] Paul Johnson, *Modern Times*, Harper & Row, 1983, p. 4

[120] Dan Barker, *Godless*, Ulysses Press, 2008, pp. 69-70

[121] C. S. Lewis, *Mere Christianity*, p. 38

[122] Christopher Hitchens and Douglas Wilson, *Is Christianity Good for the World?*, Canon Press, 2009, p. 55

[123] *Ibid.*, p. 59

[124] Quote from *Collision*, Crux Pictures, Gorilla Poet Productions, 2009

[125] William Lane Craig and Quentin Smith, *Theism, Atheism, and Big Bang Cosmology*, Oxford University Press, 1993, p. 30

[126] *Ibid.*, p. 14

[127] www.reasonablefaith.org/the-existence-of-god-and-the-beginning-of-the-universe

[128] Craig and Sinnot-Armstrong, *op. cit.*, p. 6

[129] Craig and Smith, *op. cit.*, p. 10

[130] Richard Swinburne, *Is There a God?*, Oxford University Press, 1996, pp. 48-49

[131] Bertrand Russell and F. C. Copleston, "A Debate on the Existence of God," in *Bertrand Russell on God and Religion*, Al Seckel, ed., Prometheus Books, 1986, p. 131

[132] See richarddawkins.net/articles/3626

[133] Richard Dawkins, *Climbing Mount Improbable*, Norton, 1997 (1996), chapter 5

[134] David Hume, *Dialogues Concerning Natural Religion*, Part VI

[135] *Ibid.*

[136] *Ibid.*, Part VII

[137] Stewart Goetz and Charles Taliaferro, *Naturalism*, Wm. B. Eerdmans, 2008, p. 68

[138] Hume *op. cit.*, Part XI

[139] Stephen Hawking, *A Brief History of Time*, Bantam Books, 1988, pp. 121-122.

[140] See, e.g., Richard Deem, "Evidence for the Fine Tuning of the Universe," www.godandscience.org/apologetics/designun.html

[141] Craig and Sinnot-Armstrong, *op. cit.*, p. 9

[142] Cited in Dinesh D'Souza, *What's So Great about Christianity*, p. 131

[143] George F. R. Ellis, "Does the Multiverse Really Exist?", *Scientific American*, August 2011, p. 38

[144] Craig and Sinnot-Armstrong, *op. cit.*, p. 9

[145] Dinesh D' Souza, *op. cit.*, p. 130

[146] Stephen Hawking, *op. cit.*, p. 128. This same point is made in greater detail by Victor Stenger in *The Fallacy of Fine-Tuning*, Prometheus Books, 2011, pp. 202-204

[147] Bernard Haisch, *The Purpose-Guided Universe*, New Page Books, 2010, pp. 70-72

[148] Victor Stenger, *God: the Failed Hypothesis*, Prometheus Books, 2007, pp. 148-149

[149] David Ramsay Steele, *Atheism Explained*, Open Court, 2008, p. 288n26

[150] Craig and Sinnot-Armstrong, *op. cit.*, p. 12

[151] Michael Shermer, *The Believing Brain*, St. Martin's Press, 2011, p. 153

[152] Susan Blackmore, *Dying to Live*, Prometheus Books, 1993, p. 65

[153] *Ibid.*, p. 17

[154] *Ibid.*, p. 227

[155] Keith Augustine, "The Case Against Immortality," *Skeptic*, Vol. 5, No. 2 (1997), p. 85

[156] A. J. Ayer, "What I Saw When I Was Dead," in Paul Edwards, *Immortality*, Prometheus Books, 1997, pp. 271-272

[157] Blackmore, *op. cit.*, pp. 131-133

[158] Sharon Hill, "No, this study is not evidence for 'life after death'," *SWIFT, James Randi Educational Foundation*, 8 Oct. 2014

[159] Stated during a debate between Hitchens and Tony Blair.

INDEX

Made in the USA
Coppell, TX
26 March 2021